WE ARE ALL
WATER
BABIES

Jessica Johnson
& Michel Odent

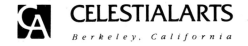

CELESTIALARTS
Berkeley, California

This book is dedicated to my
partner, Falcon, and our two sons,
Dashiell and Hugo. J.J.

Celestial Arts Publishing,
PO Box 7327,
Berkeley,
CA 94707

First published in the UK by
Dragon's World Ltd 1994

© 1995 Main text Michel Odent
© 1995 Photographs and additional text
Jessica Johnson

The photographs on pages 53 and 124 are
© Barry Lategan and John Tarrant
respectively. The photographs on pages 59
and 65 are reproduced by permission of
Michel Odent.

Library of Congress
Cataloguing-in-publication data on file with
the publisher.

ISBN 0-89087-758-0

Editor: Patricia Burgess
Designer: John Strange
DTP Manager: Keith Bambury
Editorial Director: Pippa Rubinstein

Printed in Italy

CONTENTS

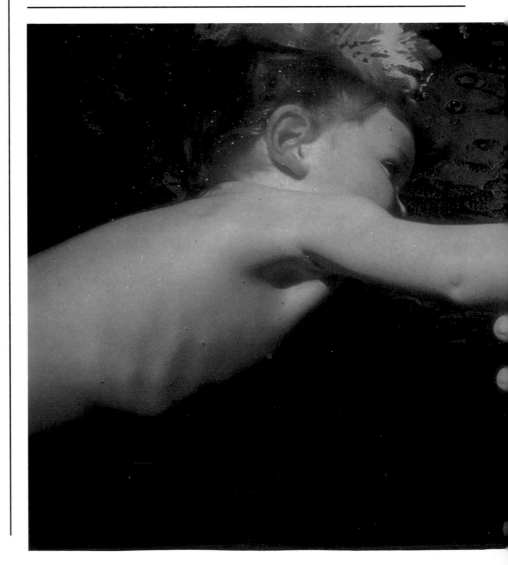

WE ARE ALL
WATER
BABIES

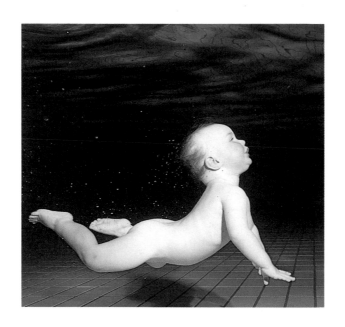

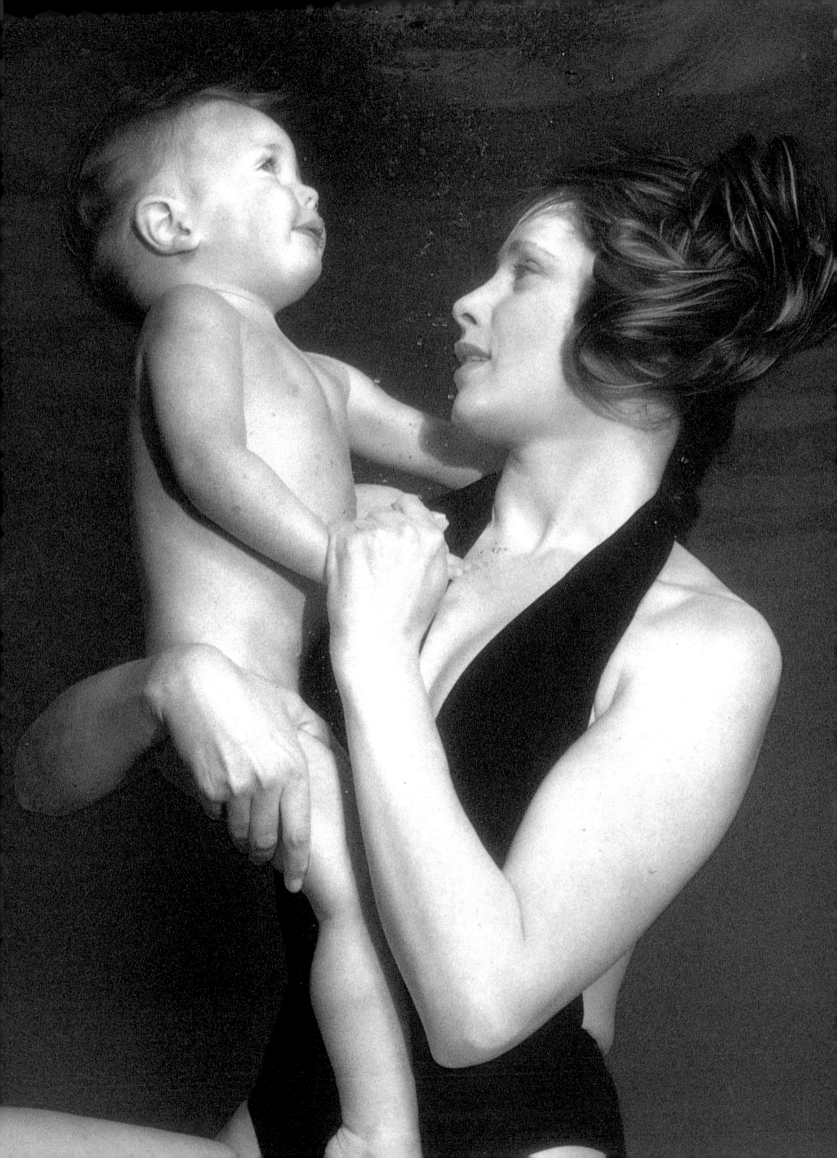

IMPORTANT
This book is not intended as an instruction manual. Parents wanting to introduce their babies to the joys of early swimming should seek the advice of an expert.

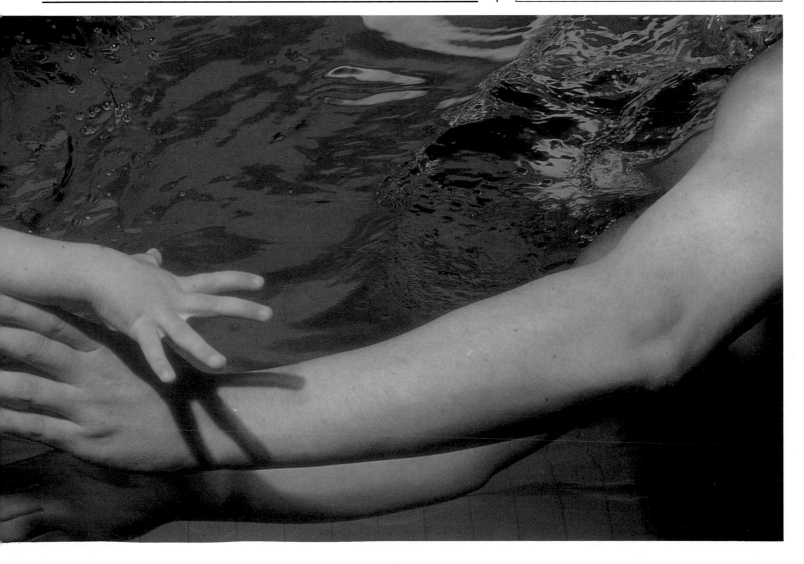

Introduction
We are all water babies

Jessica Johnson, the photographer, has learned much about the relationship between humans and water, both through her own experiences with water and from talking to many people while preparing this book. Her comments and those of her subjects appear in large quotes throughout.

' While attending a conference about dolphins in Brussels, I had time to reflect on how this book really came into being.

Dr Horace Dobbs, probably one of the most significant figures in the research on dolphins and the so-called 'Dolphin Connection', was speaking at the conference about his studies with ambassador dolphins and the effect they had on humans, particularly those suffering from depression. His research led him to found Operation Sunflower, so named after a woman saw her manic-depressive husband, Bill, swim with a dolphin and smile for the first time in 12 years. She said that he 'blossomed like a sunflower'.

Mention of sunflowers made Horace Dobbs think of the depressive painter Vincent Van Gogh, who expressed his emotions so powerfully through his paintings. Dobbs realized that the name for his new mission derived not only from Bill, but also reflected the link between art and science. He felt that the two disciplines should be encouraged to work harmoniously together and thus bring about new awarenesses and opportunities for more and more people.

In a similar way *Water Babies*, was inspired by two quite separate situations. The first related to my early diving experiences when I had to overcome my initial fear of entering the water. In complete contrast I later observed babies' total lack of fear in and under the water from birth to several months. '

The advent of paid holidays is a turning point in the history of the 20th century. I was a 6-year-old boy when the French Parliament voted for the new law. Thousands of families, including mine, had the same reflex at the same time. We went to a beach in Normandy and spent a summer week watching the waves. This human fascination for water – deeply imprinted in my memory – has come back to my conscious mind in many circumstances of my professional and private life.

I cannot find a more appropriate term than 'swimming against the tide' to describe our attitude at the state maternity hospital in Pithiviers in the 1970s. This was a time when most obstetricians were guided, even obsessed, by theories. Their basic idea was that the only way to improve birth statistics was to improve the methods of monitoring the baby during labour and to introduce increasingly sophisticated electronic machines to the delivery rooms. The electronic age in childbirth was establishing itself before any scientific evaluation had been attempted on the possible side-effects of an electronic environment during birth. Our approach in Pithiviers was exactly the opposite and therefore difficult to understand by those in the medical profession. Our priority, though simple, was paradoxically new in the field of medicine. Our primary objective was simply to make the birth as easy as possible. This led in particular to the designing of small, dimly lit, home-like birthing rooms with a relaxed atmosphere.

It was in such a context that we noticed the attraction many labouring women have towards water. They want to have a shower or bath. One winter's day I went to a shop in the high street of our town and, to the surprise of the shopkeeper, I bought an inflatable blue paddling pool. She was even more surprised when she understood that the pool was to be used in the hospital. The busy maintenance engineers at the hospital were

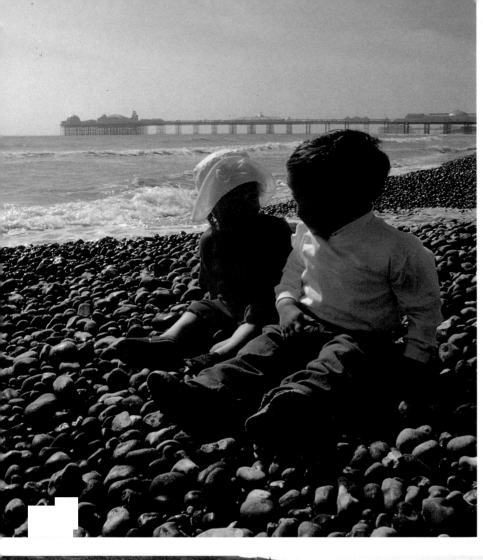

LEFT AND BELOW: *Human beings have an irresistible attraction towards the sea. The lapping or pounding of the waves can have a powerful influence on our moods.*

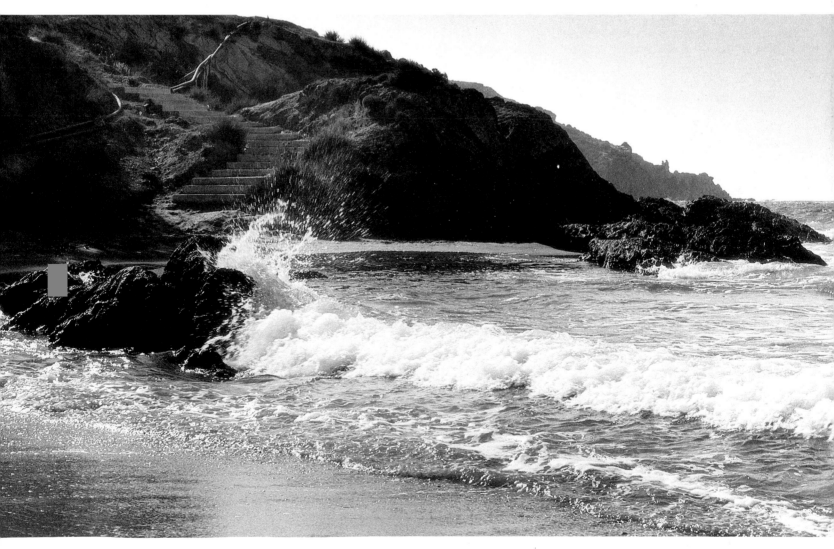

'The first encounter I had with the extraordinary technique of teaching babies to swim without the use of buoyancy aids was through my close friend Lauren Heston. Prior to becoming a teacher of 'little dippers', as she calls them, Lauren had featured in many underwater films. Her grace and beauty were matched by her great physical endurance. Lauren is able to stay under water, often at depths of up to 27m (90 ft), for long periods of time, without breathing apparatus and protective clothing. Her only air supply comes from a buddy diver at regular but sometimes lengthy intervals.

After observing and photographing the babies with Lauren's help and encouragement, I thought of producing a book that would clearly illustrate the benefits and links that water provides in our lives from birth to death.

Although I had an overall idea of the book, I could not envisage the voyage of discovery that its production would take me on and the fascinating people I would meet. Constantly welcomed and treated with warmth and hospitality by the medical profession, I realized that artist and scientist can work together successfully and productively. '

also surprised when I asked them to connect the pool to the water supply. None the less, they were incredibly zealous, postponing their daily work to perform this task, as if aware of its special importance.

This, in a nutshell, is how hospital birthing pools came about. As soon as the Pithiviers pool was installed, I was faced with the most intriguing aspects of the human fascination for water. I could tell countless stories of labouring women whose attraction towards water was so irresistible that they frustrated the best-laid plans of the staff. Women could not wait to get into the pool. As soon as the tap was turned on, they stepped in while there was no more than an inch of water at the bottom of it. This kind of impulsive, irrational behaviour was, more often than not, a sign that a series of strong and effective contractions leading to the birth of the baby would occur before the pool was filled.

From that time on I gave importance to apparently insignificant facts in daily life, looking out for the 'magic' power of water on human beings. Why is it that many people never sing or whistle, except in the bathroom when the tap is turned on? When in London on a sunny summer day, I like walking on Parliament Hill and looking at the toddlers splashing about in the paddling pool. When watching them you cannot doubt that they are in their natural element. They are euphoric. It is the kind of childish euphoria I felt after swimming among a school of dolphins in the Gulf of Mexico. It seems that both the sea and dolphins can help liberate the child inside us. That is why we so easily stop being rational when water is concerned. This knowledge can help us interpret the attitude of some obstetricians regarding the use of water during labour.

In this book Jessica's role is to reach out to the emotional side of our nature, while my role is to reach the intellect. We combine these two routes to deliver the

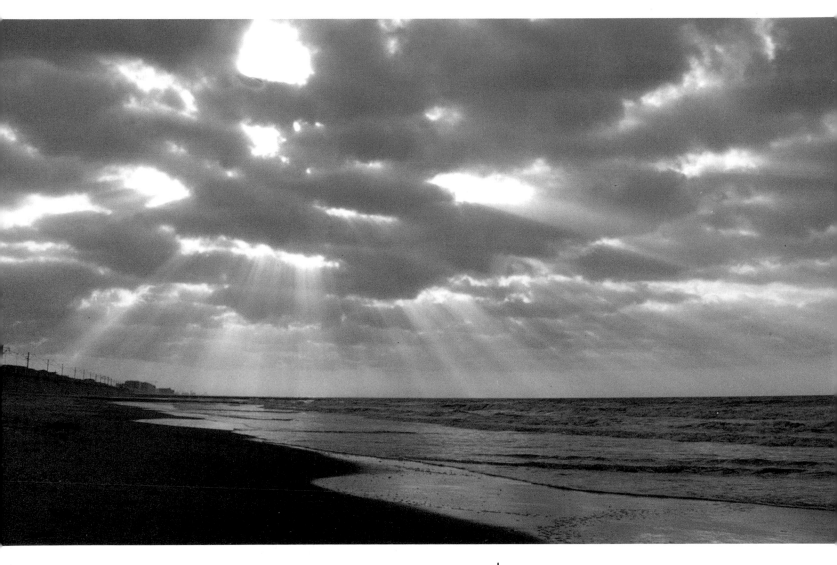

Twilight by the seashore — a peaceful scene that appeals to the deep-seated human empathy with water.

same message. The dominant theme of this book is that human beings have to live with two brains: the old, primitive, emotional brain on the one hand, and the new brain, the highly developed neocortex on the other hand. The neocortex has the power to inhibit or repress the instinctive brain in a great variety of situations, such as swimming, or giving birth, or any episode of sexual life. Water is the primary mediator or harmonizing agent in the relationship between our two brains.

After reading the book, keep it within easy reach. If you are happy or depressed, sick or old, just look again at the uplifting photographs. We are all waterbabies.

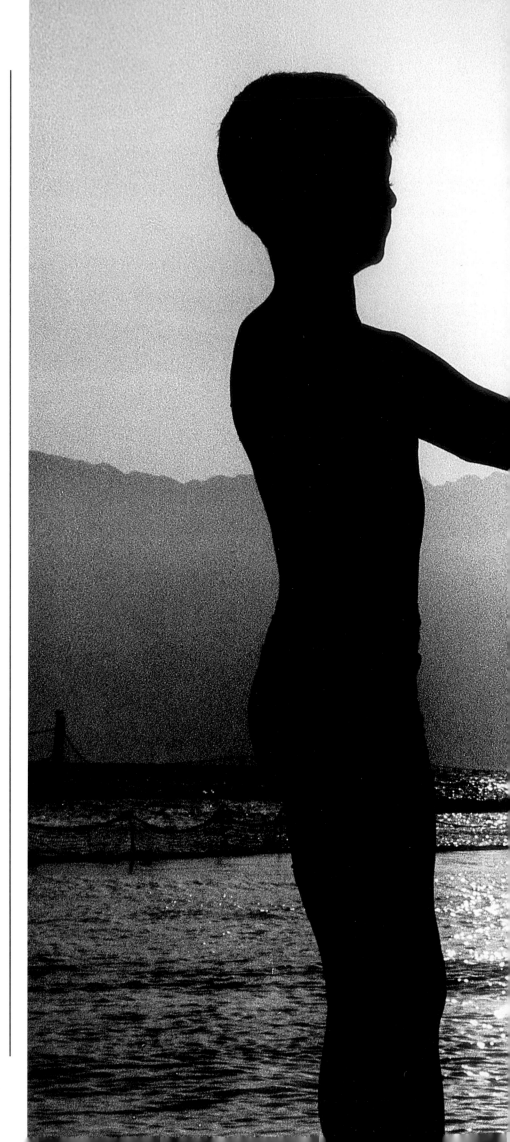

'Producing this book, with all the many people involved, particularly Michel Odent, is living testimony of the cooperation between art and science. It has changed my perception of many aspects of human life, persuaded me of the need to maintain a healthy, loving existence, and shown how water can facilitate this.

I hope this knowledge means that future generations of water babies will automatically love and respect the water that covers two-thirds of our planet, constitutes 87 per cent of our bodies and is probably the most significant element for life on Earth.

Come, take the voyage.'

Children who have experienced an early introduction to water usually have a love and respect for it, and most importantly, have the ability to get themselves out of difficulties, should they arise.

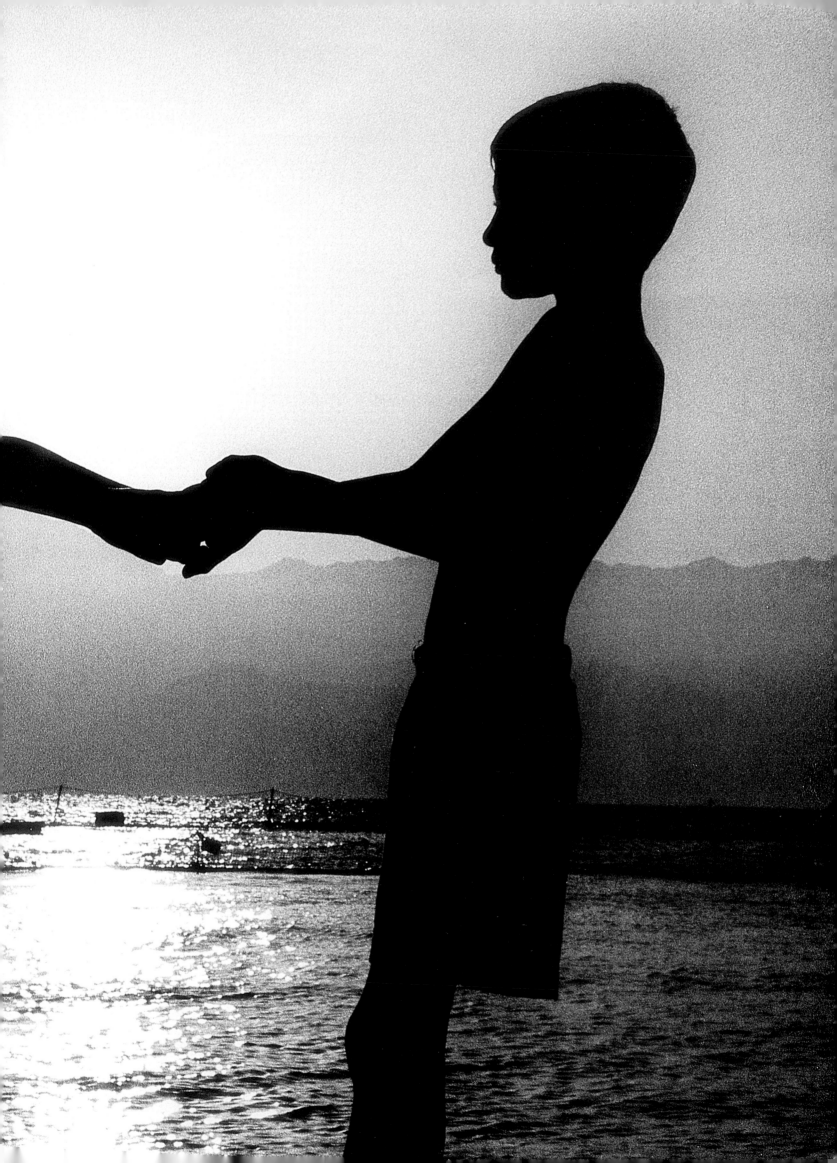

1 | What Newborn Babies Can Do

When Captain Cook discovered the Hawaiian islands in 1778, he later wrote of seeing 'neonates, floating on their backs, in the warm streams and lagoons'. In fact, wherever human beings have had quiet and warm water at their disposal, they have been able to move in water before being able to walk. Examples of this behaviour are also seen among the Yokur Indians of California and certain African tribes along the River Congo.

Until recently, the capacities of newborn babies in Western countries have generally been underestimated; indeed their aquatic capacities have been totally ignored.

The turning point came in 1939 when Dr Myrtle McGraw published her article 'Swimming Behavior of the Human Infant' in

RIGHT: *Lauren gently guides baby Hannah under the water's surface. Young babies show no sign of fear and more often than not keep their eyes open.*

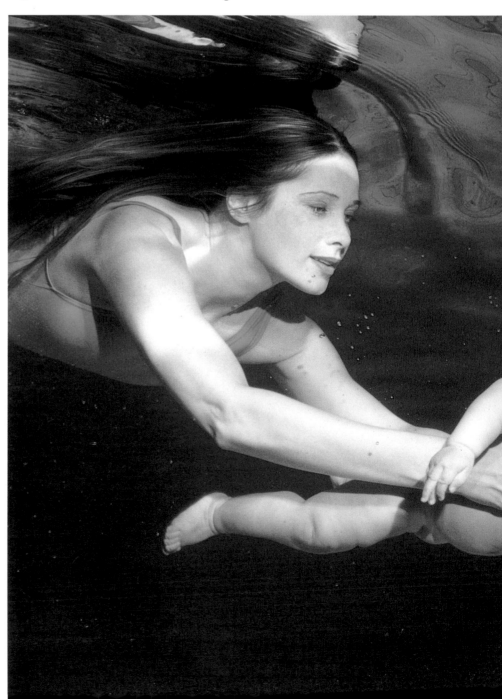

the *Journal of Pediatrics*. Dr McGraw filmed and wrote about 42 different babies during the first 2¹/₂ years of their life. She repeated observations of the same babies at different intervals, making a total of 445 observations in all. This enormous accumulation of data laid the foundations of our current knowledge of aquatic behaviour in human babies.

During the first phase of development, which concerns the first weeks of life and lasts no more than four months, the movements of the baby are striking when he/she is placed face down in water. There are rhythmical movements of flexion and extension in the legs and arms, together with swinging movements of the trunk from side to side, which propel the baby a short

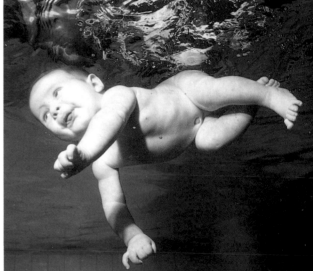

BELOW: *During their first four months babies are able to propel themselves short distances when placed face down in the water. These movements are more effective when the baby is completely submerged.*

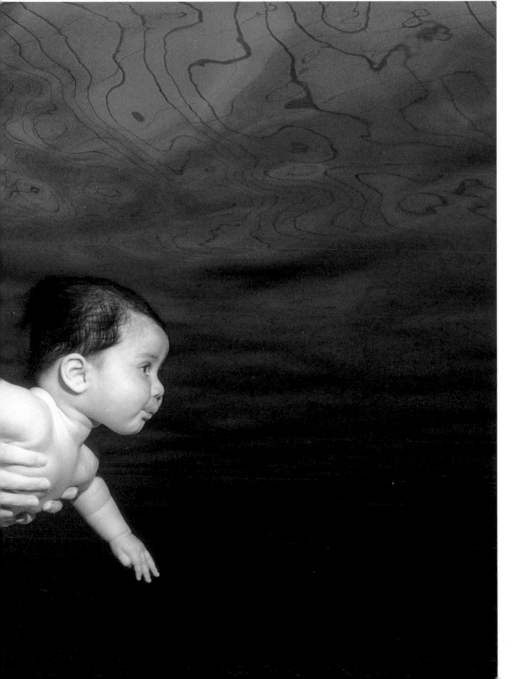

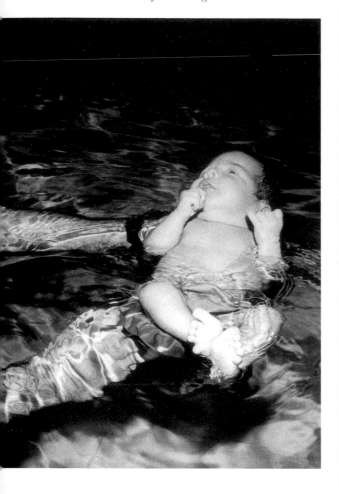

OPPOSITE: *The newborn baby is well adapted to immersion and will automatically hold his/her breath when submerged. This is known as the 'diving reflex.*

distance through the water. These movements are better organized and more pronounced when the baby is submerged. This is another outstanding feature which arises from Dr McGraw's pioneering study: the human newborn baby is perfectly adapted to immersion and automatically holds his/her breath when submerged. The newborn baby does not cough or show distress after immersion. The swimming movements and the control of breathing are two behaviours which tend to reinforce each other: when the baby is in the same position in water but supported under the chin, the swimming movements are not well organized.

After babies are 4 months or older, the movements become disorganized. Often the babies are quite inactive when supported under the chin, and when submerged tummy down, they tend to rotate on to their backs. Then they appear to struggle, as if trying to clutch the hand of an adult. They sometimes swallow large amounts of water during this stage and are often coughing when their head emerges from the water.

Towards the beginning of the second year the baby recovers organized movements which can propel his/her body through the water. But these movements are less automatic than during the first weeks; they are purposeful movements in order to reach the edge of the pool. Dr McGraw noticed that at no time did any baby raise its head above the water to breathe.

The three distinct phases of development so far described are easy to recognize when babies are placed face down. This is not

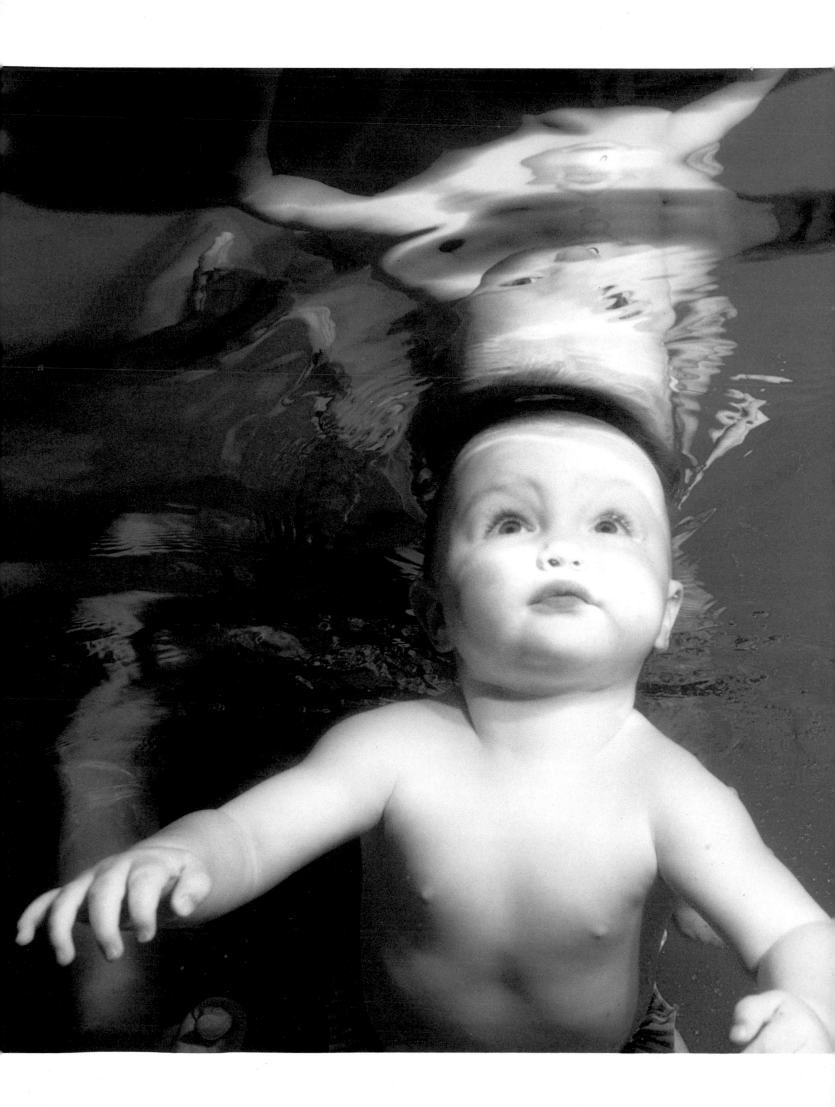

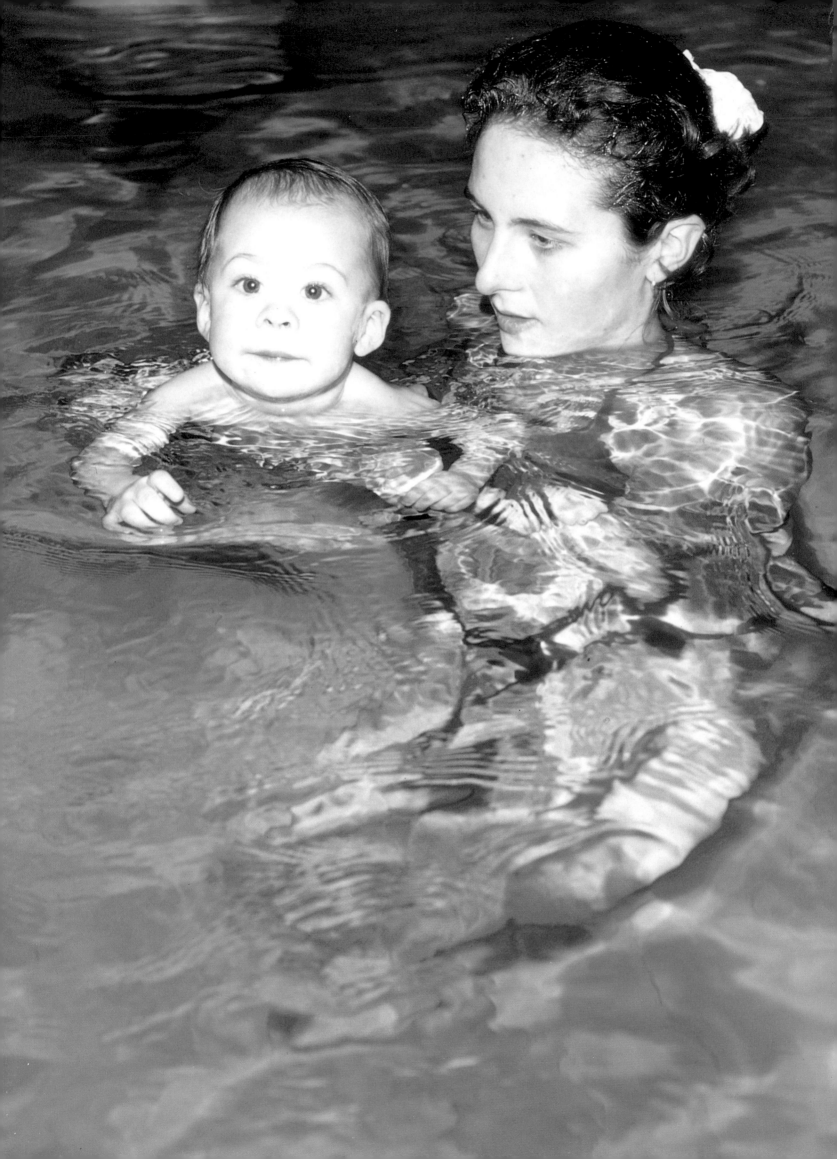

the case when babies are placed on their backs. Then they tend to struggle whatever their age and do not rotate to be on their tummy. Dr McGraw made her breakthrough discovery in understanding the swimming behaviour of human babies because she was the first to study babies immersed face down.

Dr McGraw's work is important for two reasons: first she gave a detailed description of the three phases of development; second, she gave an interpretation of the aquatic behaviour of babies — namely, the complex relationship between the most primitive structures of the brain and the most recent ones. Her interpretation made it clear that the automatic swimming behaviour observed during the first weeks of life belongs to a framework of early reflexes which are totally under the control of the primitive part of the brain. Some months after birth the 'new brain', the so-called neocortex, develops dramatically and tends to take control. There is a difficult period of transition when the neocortex is strong enough to inhibit the primitive reflexes, but too weak to make purposeful behaviour well organized. When the neocortex has reached a certain degree of maturity, the new mechanisms are settled and the child needs training to stay face down, as he/she now has a tendency to maintain an upright position.

Although Dr McGraw's detailed study of swimming behaviours went only up to the age of $2^1/_2$ years, she noted that most children of 5 or 6 tend to keep vertical when learning to swim — probably an adaptive response in order to keep the head above water. The ability to stay on one's tummy in water is a definite phase in learning to swim. Dr McGraw's interpretations are essential in understanding that human beings have not really lost their instincts, namely those behaviours controlled by the primitive parts of the brain. These behaviours are simply repressed, but they can reappear in certain circumstances — for example, when the cerebral hemispheres are damaged by accident or disease. The relationship between the primitive brain and the new brain is fundamental to our understanding of human behaviour. During the birth process, for example, the primitive brain cannot work properly and release the necessary hormones if the neocortex does not relinquish control. In this case we'll see how water can help labouring women to reach a particular state of consciousness, which many describe as 'going to another planet'.

No doubt many readers will be wondering how Dr McGraw and her researchers could simply 'observe' the struggling movements of the babies, the difficulties in controlling respiration and the considerable ingestion of water? We must assume that the study was conducted by professionals who had great experience of

OPPOSITE: *Babies rapidly gain confidence in the water, particularly if the primary instructor is the mother.*

BELOW: *This 10-month-old baby is happy and confident under water with Lauren.*

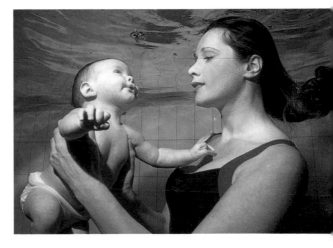

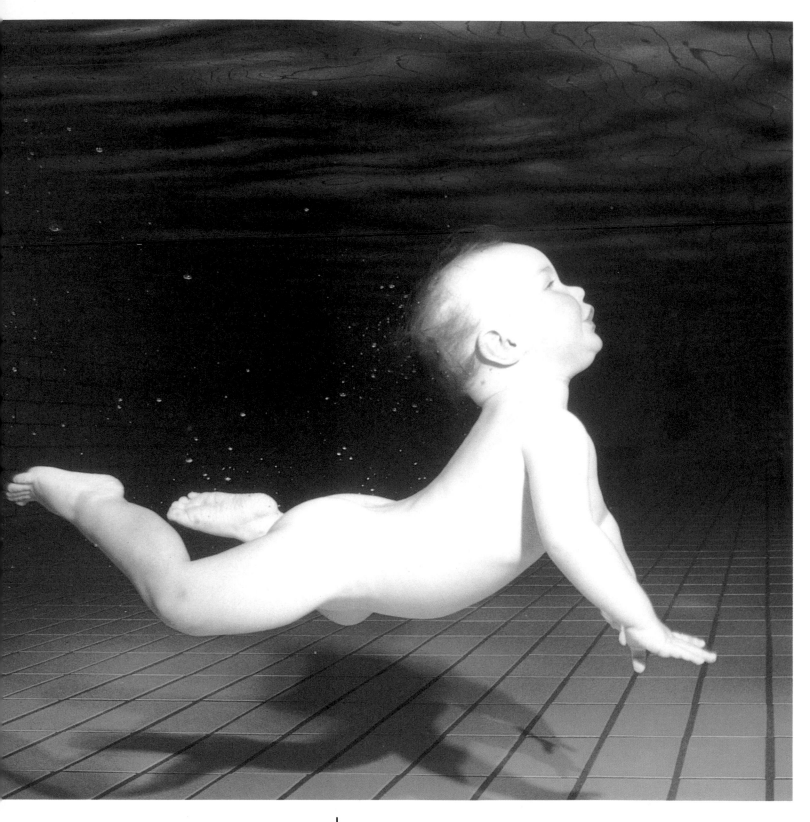

Baby Rachel shows no distress as she is submerged; her mother is close at hand to guide her gently to the surface.

OPPOSITE: *As infants grow older, their movements become more powerful as they propel themselves from one destination to another.*

babies and who knew the acceptable limit between observation and action. Fifty years later the point is to acknowledge the scientific breakthrough the research represents.

Our current awareness of the coexistence of two brains that do not develop in parallel can shed a new light on human phenomena. Sudden Infant Death Syndrome, for example, is specifically human and most commonly occurs around the age of 4 months — the critical period when the neocortex is assuming dominance and the final breathing control mechanisms are not yet completely settled.

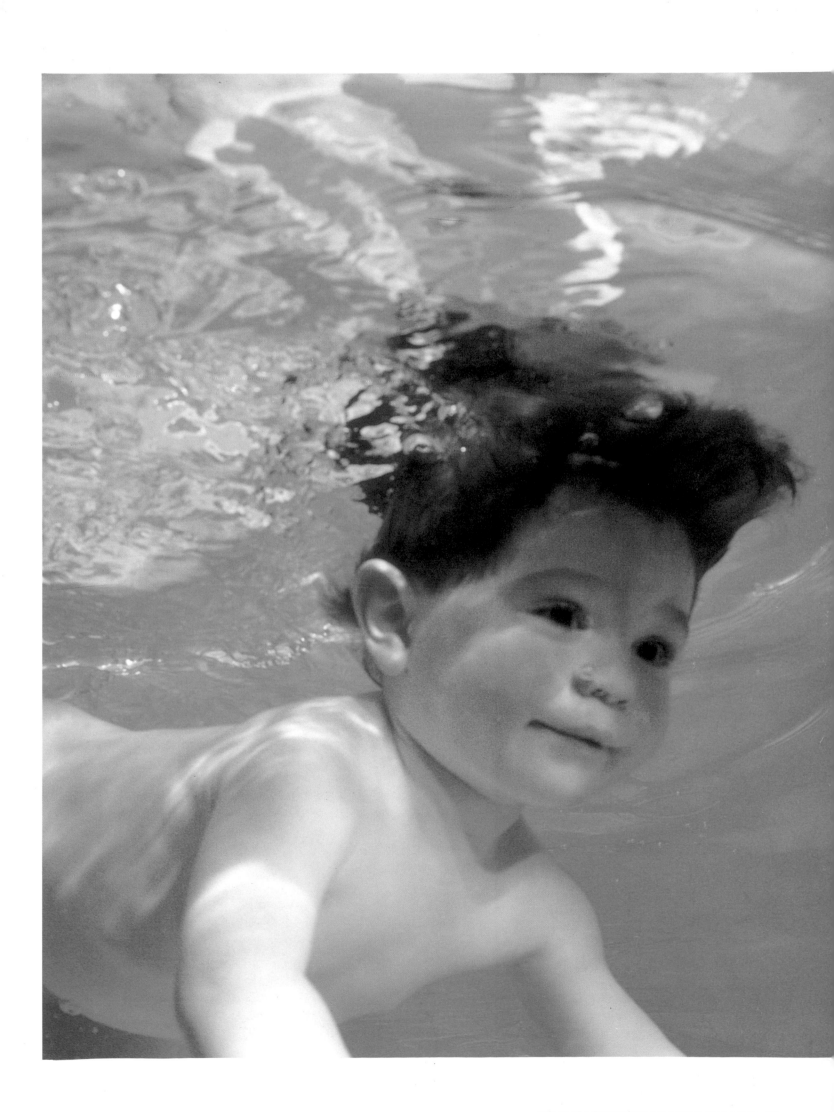

2 | Babies and Swimming Instructors

'Watching Lauren as a swimming instructor of infants simply reinforces for me what Michel states in this chapter. As a person she is calm and confident – important qualities for a teacher, as they are passed on to the parents, who in turn pass them on to their children. Lauren runs frequent classes for up to five babies, each accompanied by one or both parents. The groups are divided according to experience – one group devoted to those new to water, usually starting at around 5 weeks, and another to older infants with mixed abilities, aged from 3 to 18 months.

The first thing that struck me while watching Lauren's classes was the number of parents who were themselves nervous of the water. However, the combination of warm, shallow water and Lauren's gentle encouragement soon helped the parents to relax and feel at ease with their surroundings.'

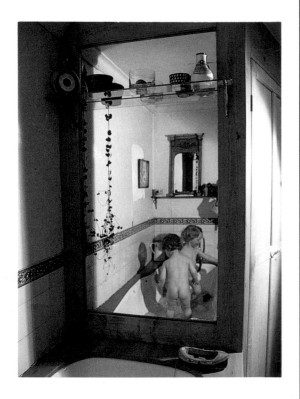

Since Dr McGraw's authoritative study, physiologists have learnt more about 'airway protective reflexes' and different aspects of the 'diving reflex', including the fact that the heart slows down. But during the past four decades the real breakthroughs have been practical rather than scientific, allowing thousands of babies all over the world to enjoy swimming activities. The general public became aware of the aquatic capacities of babies thanks to the work of devoted pioneers such as Virginia Hunt Newman in California. Her book, *Teaching an Infant to Swim*, published more than 30 years ago, is still a classic. She was the main organizer of the World Aquatic Baby Conference at the University of California in Los Angeles in September 1993, which brought together swimming instructors from all over the world. Particularly interesting was the fact that these experts came from a great variety of backgrounds: sport, medicine, psychology, nursing, anthropology...

During this five-day conference I watched dozens of videos of young babies propelling themselves through water with their eyes wide open. All of them were expressing the same pleasure and enjoyment of the water. The common points between what the swimming instructors had to say were striking. The behaviour of young babies under water is cross-cultural: all of them kick the water in exactly the same way. Moreover, the instructors, who spend a great part of their life with babies, tend to use the same kind of vocabulary, whatever their mother tongue and the country where they practise. The terms most often used were 'water adjustment', 'water familiarization', 'water fun', 'exploration' and 'games'. Notably absent were words such as 'swimming', 'drownproofing' and 'waterproofing'.

The consensus of opinion is that the primary teacher should be the mother, who cultivates the baby's adaptation to water. If the mother is not comfortable in water, another familiar adult can replace her. However, most mothers need to be reassured and even guided by an experienced specialized swimming instructor. John Bainbridge, chairman of the infant committee of the National Swim School Association (USA), has compiled some simple suggestions for babies up to the age of 2 months. He recommends starting instruction in the bath at home. The water should be at body temperature (37°C) and the baby placed with his/her head close to your heart. The water should cover the baby's ears. This position should be held for a couple of minutes while you touch and caress the baby. If he/she begins to fuss (very rare in this position and at this age), change the position, offer the breast and repeat the previous position. Then sit up and place the baby in front of you, supporting the head and upper back with one hand.

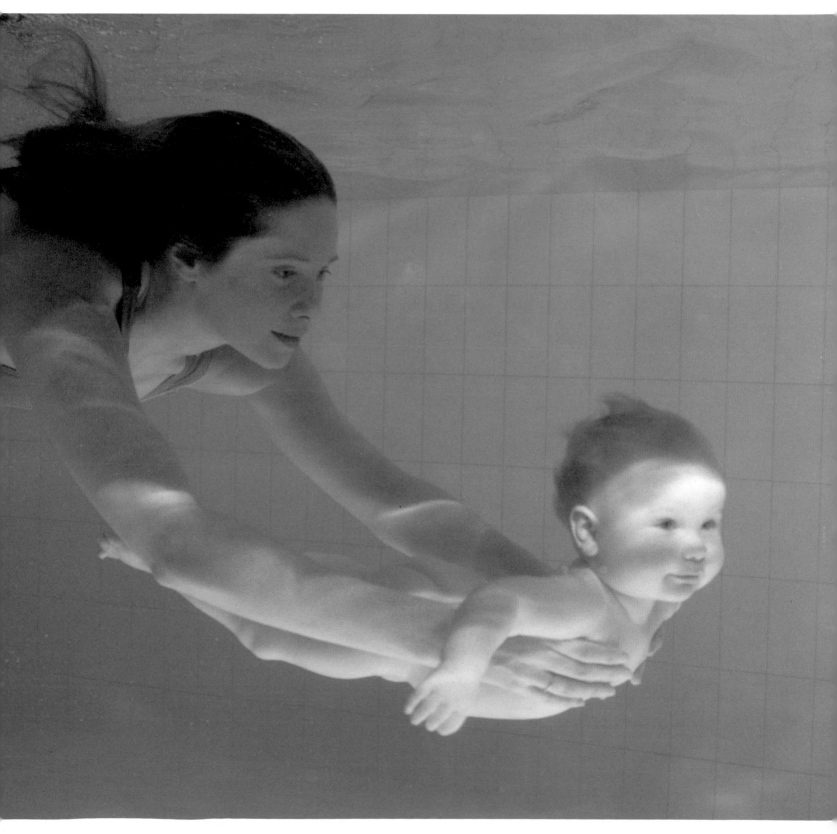

Your other hand can support or caress his/her body. The next step is to move the baby out in front of you in 'S' patterns. Babies love motion and the feel of water flowing over their skin. You should change direction from time to time, first floating the baby with the feet away from you and then facing you.

The first bath should last 5 to 10 minutes. Increase the time gradually up to about 30 minutes over the first month. Always leave the water before the baby becomes fussy. The bath can be repeated every day. Reduce the water temperature gradually from 37ºC to 32ºC, which will be the pool temperature, so that the baby will be ready for pool time, which can be around the age of 2 months. The baby can stay in the pool for 20 to 30 minutes

'Repetition and key word association are used to encourage the baby's natural 'diving reflex' that will enable it to go under the water successfully. At the beginning, Lauren uses a doll to demonstrate the correct way to hold the baby and how to scoop water in the palm of the hand and pour it gently over the baby's face while saying 'Ready, go'.'

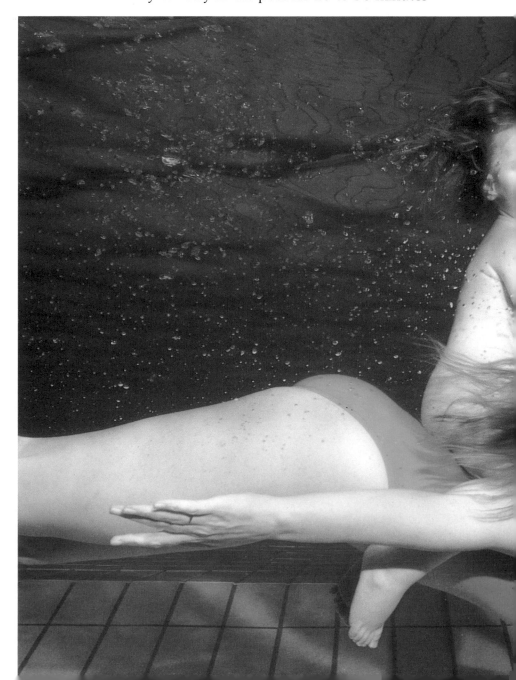

several times a week. John Bainbridge makes the following suggestions for pool time:

● Begin by supporting the baby in the back position with the baby's head on your shoulder.

● Place your cheek close to the baby and talk or sing while you move about the pool. The water must be above the baby's ears.

● After a couple of minutes, hold the baby with your hands, keeping the water over the ears, but offer less support so that the baby can feel its natural buoyancy.

● When you feel it is the right time to work on breath control, place the baby face down, wrapping your hands around it so that the thumbs are near the nipples.

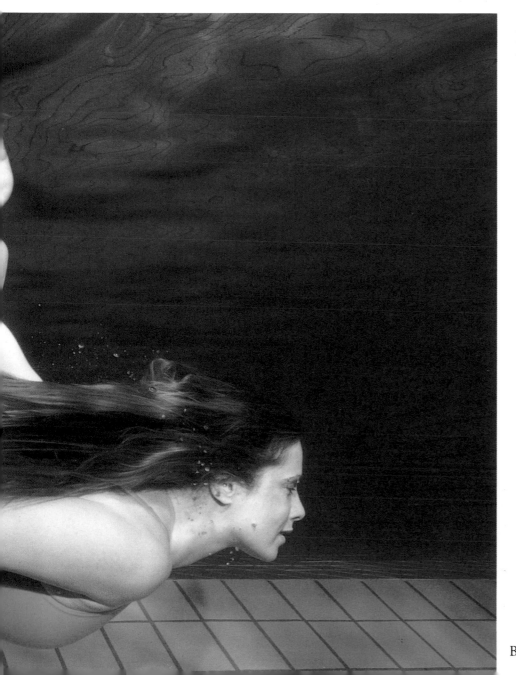

Lauren runs her baby swimming classes under the name of 'Little Dippers'. Here she is giving Claire an underwater ride on her back.

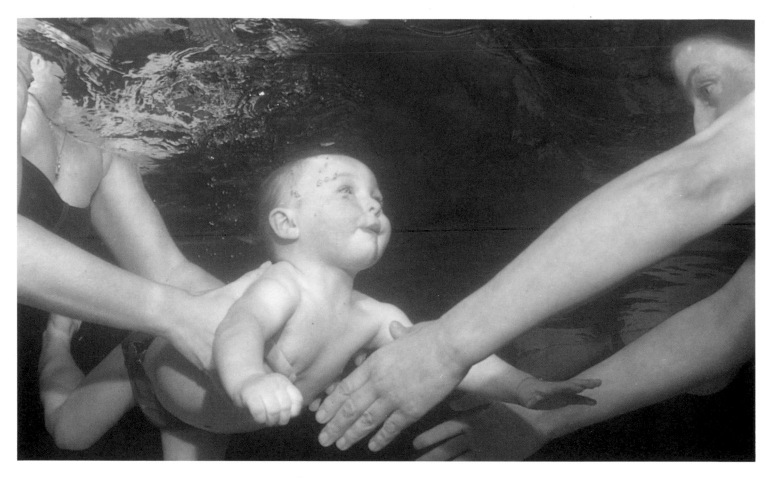

ABOVE: *It is generally accepted that the primary instructor should be the mother, but that doesn't mean that fathers and other familiar adults are excluded. No matter which carer accompanies an infant, it is essential to have the guidance and reassurance of an experienced instructor.*

OPPOSITE: *Babies are soon quite happy to enjoy a little independence under a watchful eye.*

'When the babies are ready for their first submersion, everyone gathers in a large circle. Lauren does the first submersion with each baby because even the most confident of mothers can feel a little apprehensive.

Standing in the middle of the circle, holding the child close to her, she issues the command words while pouring a little water over the baby's face. Then, holding the baby in front of her at arm's length, she says, 'Ready, go' and the baby has its first submersion. Two or three seconds pass — you can almost hear all the parents holding their breath as the baby is guided under water and back up to Lauren's shoulder. Short cheers and cooing follow, which instil calmness and confidence in both parents and the babies.

Lauren repeats this process with all the remaining children, then the parents themselves have a go. '

● Walk backwards, looking at the baby, and when you catch his/her eyes, you start what will become a ritual. For example, say the baby's name, and then 'Ready...go!' As you say 'ready', lift the baby up (not all the way out), raise your head, and when you say 'go', put your head down and submerge the baby.

● With the baby's head completely submerged (John Bainbridge insists on this point), continue walking backwards and slowly draw the baby towards your shoulder. The underwater time, keeping the baby face down, should not be more than 2 or 3 seconds.

John Bainbridge explains his strategy as follows. When you walk backwards, water is less likely to go up the nose. When you lift the baby up, the whole body is given a signal that submersion is coming. When you lower your head, you give a visual signal that submersion is coming. When you give the commands, you add an auditory signal. If the head is not totally submerged, the baby will get mixed messages and might sniff or gulp water. If the submersion lasts two to three seconds, the baby has a chance to hold its breath. When you draw the baby to the shoulder, you indicate that the baby needs to recognize the shoulder as the focal point he/she is travelling to. As babies learn by association and repetition, it is important to give the same signals each time.

The submersions should be performed in series, starting with one or two per session. Stop the series if the baby is having difficulties or starts crying. Distract the baby with something funny. Start another series of submersions a few minutes later. There should be a break of 15 seconds between each submersion. Do not change the baby's position. If the baby is achieving good breath control, you can increase the duration of each series of submersions.

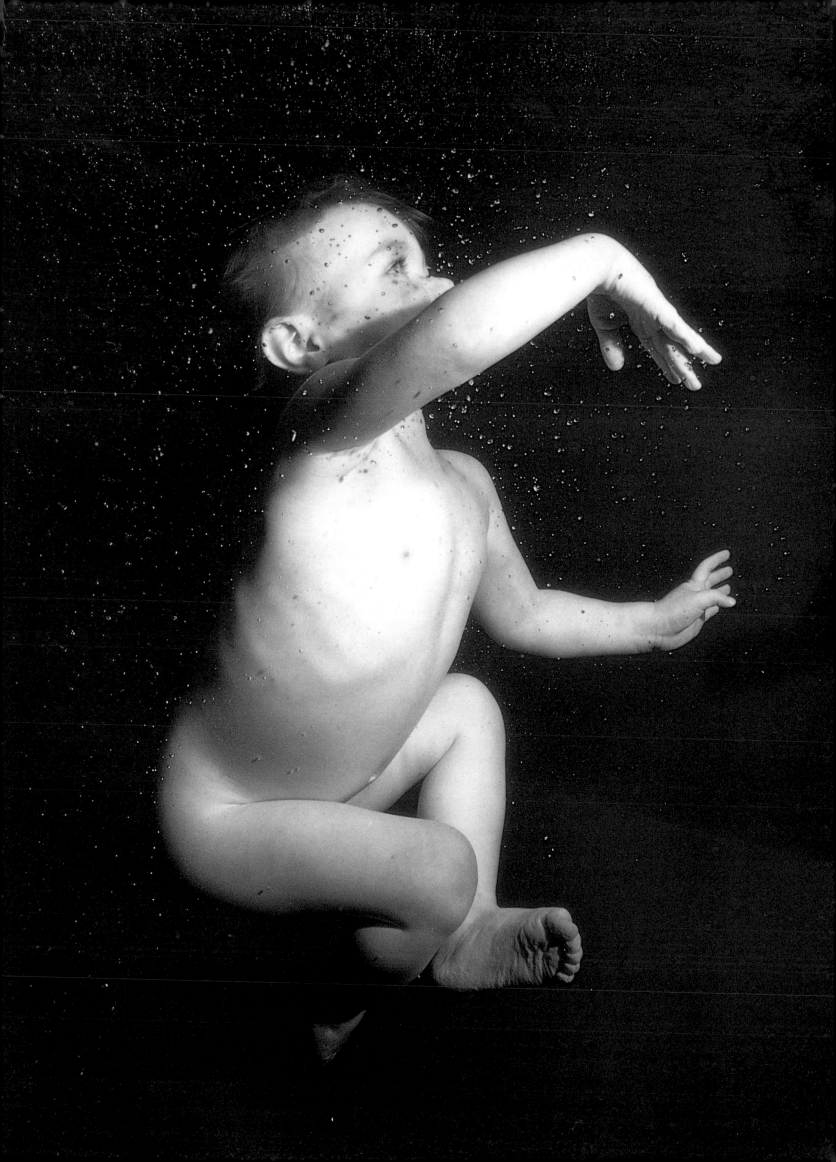

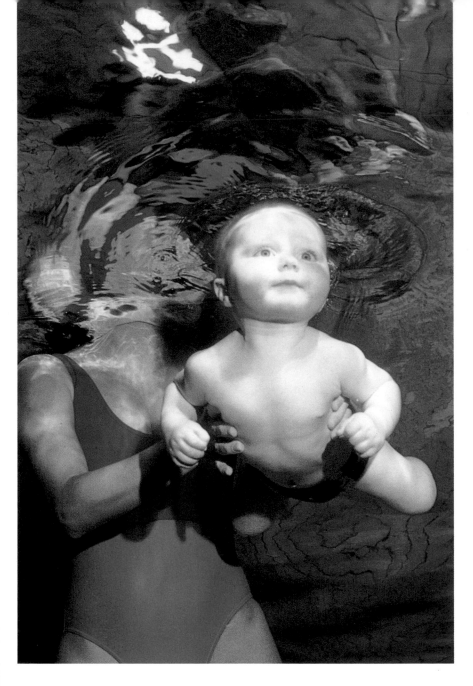

Constant repetition and key word association in the early stages will prepare the baby for submersion.

❝ Swimming lessons are not simply about submersions — parents and babies are also encouraged to play. The babies seem so contented as they learn to explore their feeling of weightlessness — tiny little arms and hands splashing and little legs kicking with pleasure. The inflatables in the water also act as good focal points for the babies to train their eyes on. ❞

Approximately two-thirds of each lesson should be spent with the baby on its back. If the baby becomes restless, pick him/her up, change positions and try again a few minutes later. Let the baby hold a soft toy. Look down at him/her, be expressive, suck his/her toes and constantly move about the pool. Do not repeat the submersions if the baby is sniffing or coughing when surfacing, or appears to be drinking when under the water. (The last is rare at the age of 2 or 3 months.)

All these suggestions and recommendations concern the easy and safe phase, up to the age of 3 to 4 months, when the aquatic behaviour of the baby is controlled by the primitive structures of the brain, meaning that the early reflexes are still present. After the age of 4 months the behaviour of the baby becomes much more complex. Then it is difficult to transmit simple suggestions. The role of an experienced swimming instructor, who can adapt to every child, becomes more important.

Many associations of swimming instructors have published guidelines for children under the age of 3. Those issued by the National Swimming School Association (USA) are a good synthesis of them all and should be consulted by parents who are concerned with the choice of swimming pool and teacher.

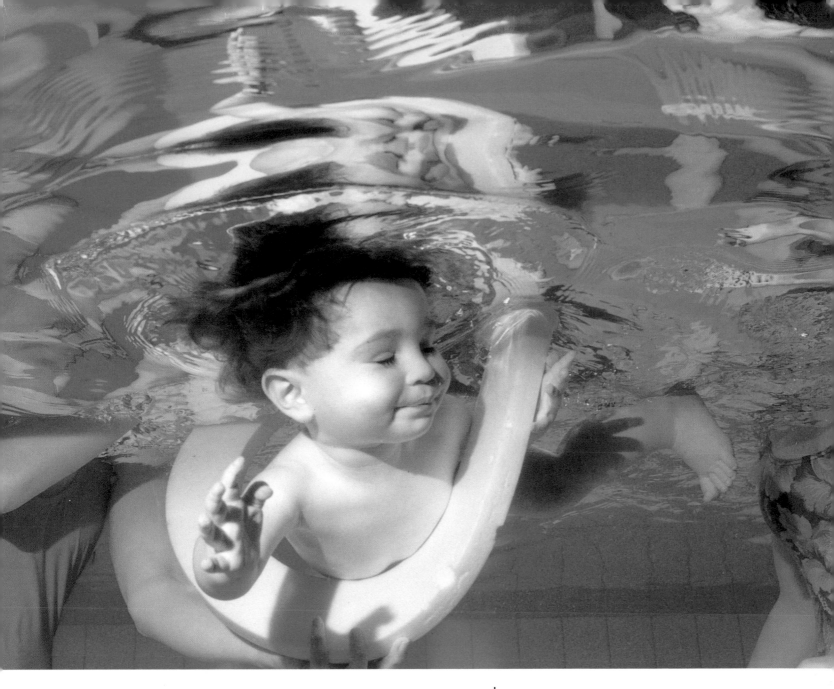

Simple submersions soon lead on to underwater games, like swimming through hoops.

● 'A child's swim lesson or water orientation requires the involvement and education of the primary caretaker or responsible adult who is accompanying the child.'

● 'The learning atmosphere should be safe and happy with loving teachers.'

● 'Instruction should be carried out by qualified teachers who have special training and experience in infant swim education, child development, and water safety.'

Other points concern, the water temperature, water purity and children with known medical problems,. There are also recommendations regarding the clothing young children should wear. The final guideline relates to 'procedures such as face submersions', which should be limited in both duration and number. Sessions should last no longer than 30 minutes.

Any discussion of swimming instructors would be incomplete without considering the work of Igor Tcharkovsky in Russia. His name first became widely known when Western visitors to the then Soviet Union came back with wonderful stories of pregnant women swimming with dolphins and of babies being born in the Black Sea. He was also well known as a pioneer of water births at home. Being neither doctor nor midwife, he was a rather

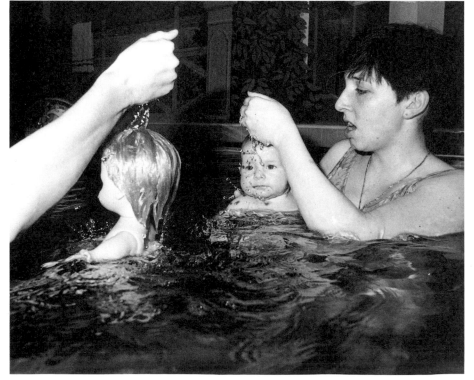

'After a few months there is a marked difference in the babies. Their movements are far more pronounced and their kicking motions under the water become more defined. After several months the difference is astonishing. Parents and babies seem totally at home in the water. The babies jump from the side of the pool, often going right under before kicking and rising to the surface and propelling themselves back to the edge of the pool. Under water their eyes are always open and they seem genuinely happy as they propel their little bodies towards their mother or father.

If a parent and child continue this practice, it will be only a matter of time before the children are swimming long before the recommended starting age of 5 years. As many drownings in the UK involve children under 5, Lauren's classes include training in water safely so that parent and child learn to respect the dangers as well as the pleasures of water. This means that the babies have a greater chance of rescuing themselves should they ever get into difficulties.'

With the aid of a doll, Lauren shows a mother how to begin accustoming her child to the water.

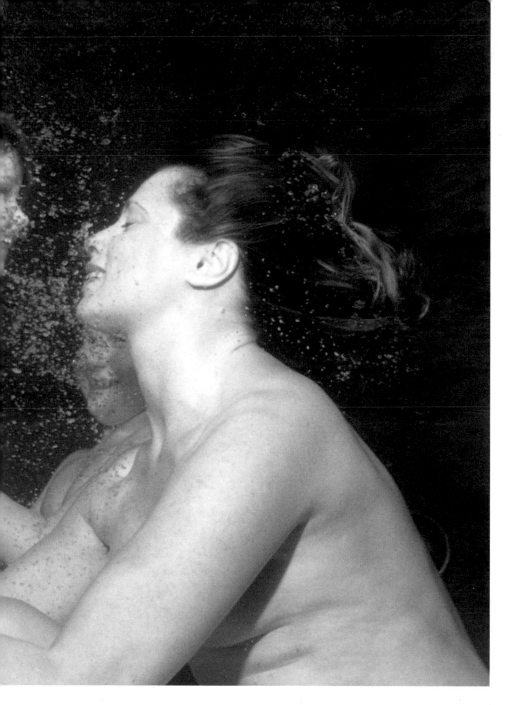

The bond between mother and baby is greatly enhanced by swimming together, as it builds up mutual trust and confidence.

mysterious figure, whose mystery was cultivated and reinforced by journalists and travellers to the Soviet Union.

In 1989 Igor made his first visit to the West. I welcomed him at Liverpool Street Station in London at the end of a 48-hour trip from Moscow. This visit marked the end of a wonderful legend because Igor's methods were considered by Westerners to be too harsh. He did not hesitate to take a one- or two-day-old baby from the arms of its mother and subject it immediately to a long underwater session. The baby learned to take a short breath every so often when Igor twisted its neck so that the nose and mouth could reach the surface. At the end of the session the baby was exhausted, discharged faeces and fell asleep. Little wonder, then, that Igor's training techniques were described as 'torture' and that London mothers refused to accept his methods.

Like many legendary people, Tcharkovsky never wrote about his work or amassed any records, so his contribution is difficult to assess. Suffice it to say that the criticisms of his attitude are at least partly counterbalanced by the fact that he helped raise awareness of the close relationship between human beings and water.

3 | Babies and Parents

'This is good for my baby.' This is what many mothers feel when their baby is in water: all they are concerned about is whether they are happy and having fun. But there are other parents who wish to know more about the effects of early aquatic activities on different aspects of development. Word of mouth and the desire to learn from other parents has led to swimming programmes being developed in many countries. Parents of swimming babies are often evangelical in explaining the benefits of early swimming – their baby is more healthy, more intelligent, more independent, more this and more that...

This type of testimonial still does not provide enough information or reassurance for some parents, particularly fathers. (Why mostly fathers?) They want to know about systematic research and expected benefits. These parents want to hear about the findings of such studies as that conducted by Liselott Diem in Cologne, Germany. This study involved observing 165 children over a period of two years. The children were divided into six groups according to when they commenced swimming (third month, or 2·4 years, or not at all) and according to any gymnastic

RIGHT: *Lucia and Lucas enjoy the extra closeness they experience through swimming together.*

OPPOSITE: *Water is a natural element for babies who are introduced to swimming at an early age.*

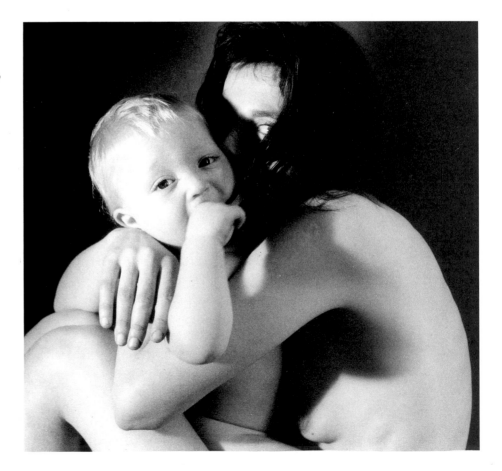

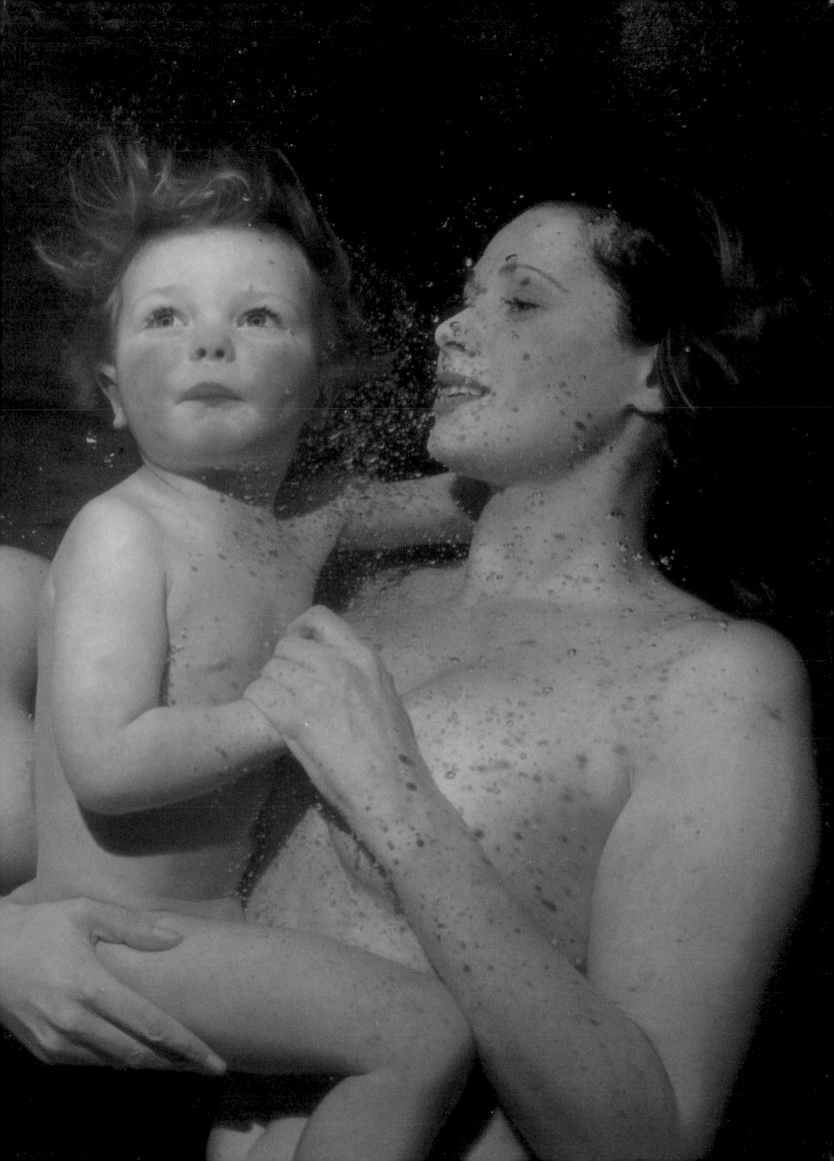

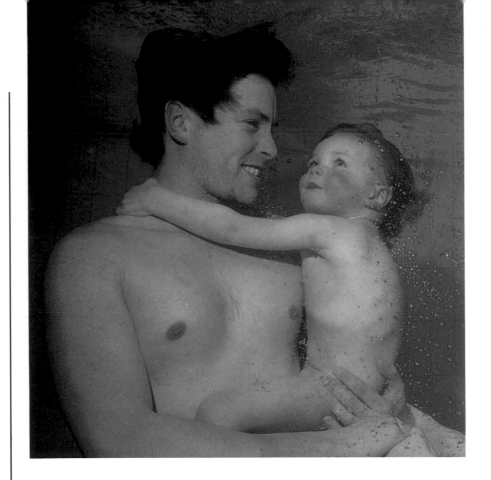

RIGHT AND OPPOSITE: *Many parents are discovering the benefits that early swimming programmes offer, not only for their children but also for their own well-being. Various studies have shown that infants who participate in regular water activities, particularly from the third month of their lives, frequently show advanced levels of physical development, stamina and learning skills.*

' The experiences of Lorraine and her three daughters clearly show the benefits of an early introduction to swimming.

At 19 Lorraine had her first child, Sarah. She took her swimming every two weeks from around the age of 6 months, using buoyancy aids such as water wings and rubber rings. Sarah, however, would bite them causing punctures, and Lorraine had to replace them virtually each time.

Her second daughter, Claire, was introduced to the water around the age of 4 months, again using buoyancy aids. It was around that time that Lorraine read a magazine article about the techniques of teaching babies to swim without the use of such aids. Claire started these classes at the relatively late age of 10 months, but from the beginning she was a natural, lying face down quite happily and often letting her body glide towards the bottom of the pool. By 15 months she could jump into the pool, submerge, turn and propel herself through the water. If she was under water and felt she needed assistance, she would simply shake her head vigorously from side to side.

What seemed so unusual about Claire was that despite starting submersions late in life, she showed a naturally strong 'diving reflex' that was clearly instinctive rather than taught. '

training they had received (from the age of 3·6 years or not at all). The control group was made up of children who did not swim and had no gymnastic training. Each group was evaluated at the beginning of the study to establish its level of motor development (balancing, running, long jumping, trampoline jumping and so on). Also built into the study were tests of ability and performance, methods for controlling motor abilities, methods for testing social behaviours, and personality diagnosis. Both parents were interviewed about their style of child rearing, education goals and expectations, and role satisfaction. Mother-child interaction was observed and analysed in particular situations.

These investigations were carried out on three separate occasions using exactly the same methods and experimenters. The repeated testing provided extensive data which was statistically processed. More than 70 videotapes were recorded and could be watched by independent judges. The results were that the 'swimming children' were found to be ahead of their contemporaries in all tested areas. Those who took part in baby swimming from the third month of their lives fared particularly well in each case. Where intellectual capacities were concerned, early swimmers showed higher intelligence values with all the tests used. In social skills 'swimming children' appeared more willing to make contact and adjusted themselves better within a group of contemporaries. They were more independent, less timid and could cope better with new and strange situations.

A Finnish study, conducted at the Department of Physical Education in Jyväskylä, focused more on the motor development of children observed over a period of nine months. The children participating in the study were randomly divided into a control group (no swimming at all) and an experimental group (swimming programme twice a week). The babies in the experimental group were ahead in the criteria for measuring the extension of their

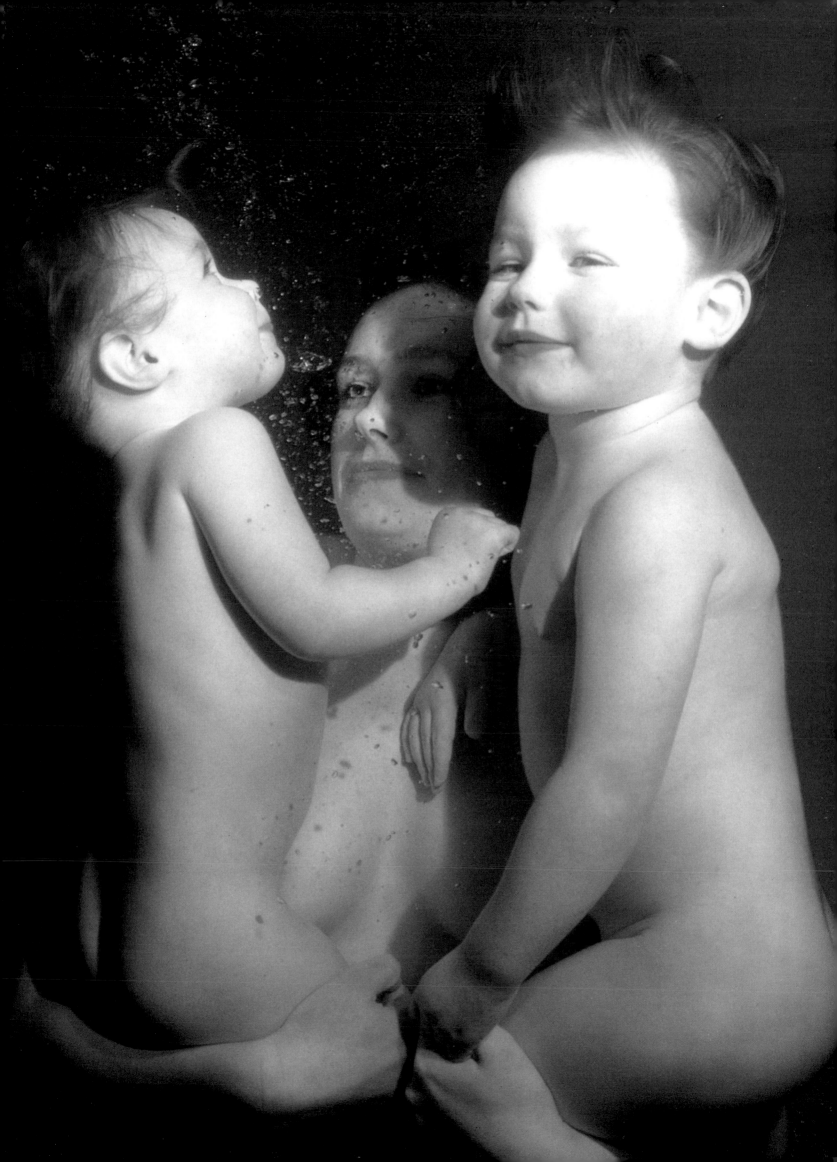

' Lorraine's third daughter, Rachel, first went to the pool when she was 8 weeks. This visit included her first submersion and she seemed completely at ease. She particularly liked lying on her back, completely still, listening to the various sounds around her. At the age of 7 months, she and two other infants were chosen to feature in an advertising campaign. Before filming began, Rachel had a full medical and the doctor was impressed to find that she had a slow and pronounced heartbeat for a baby of her age. She also won the applause of the cameraman because she was so calm and happy in the water.

Lorraine believes that their shared water activities have given her family greater closeness. Even bath times were special, right from the start. 'Whereas most families sit around the table to talk, our family would jump in the bath!' Once in the pool, they dart around, surrounded by tiny bubbles, excitement and happiness evident in their bodies and faces. '

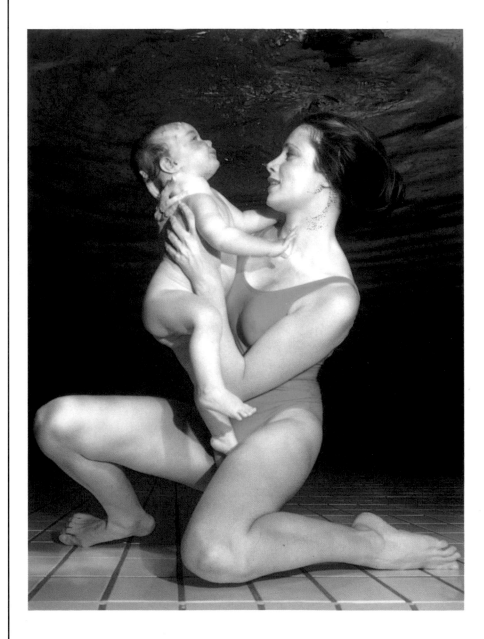

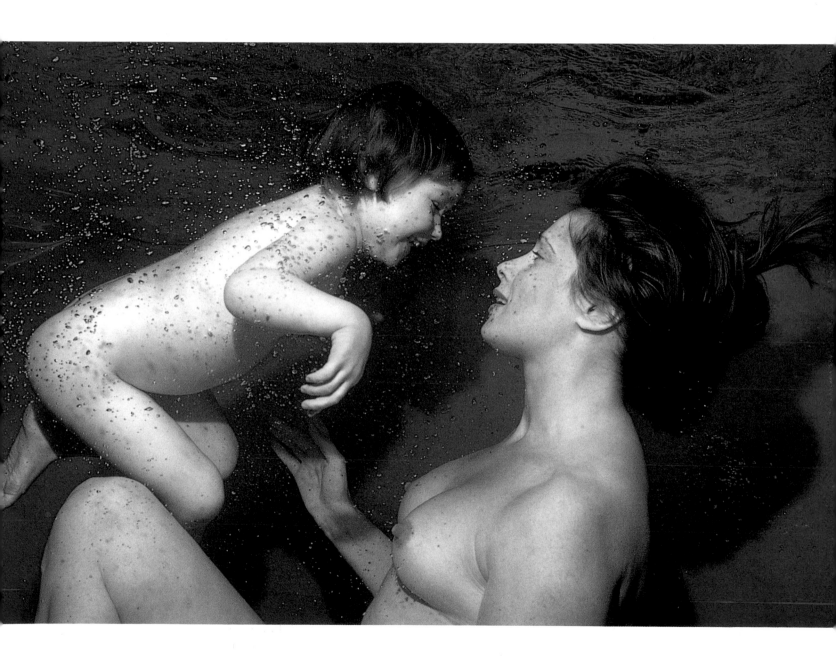

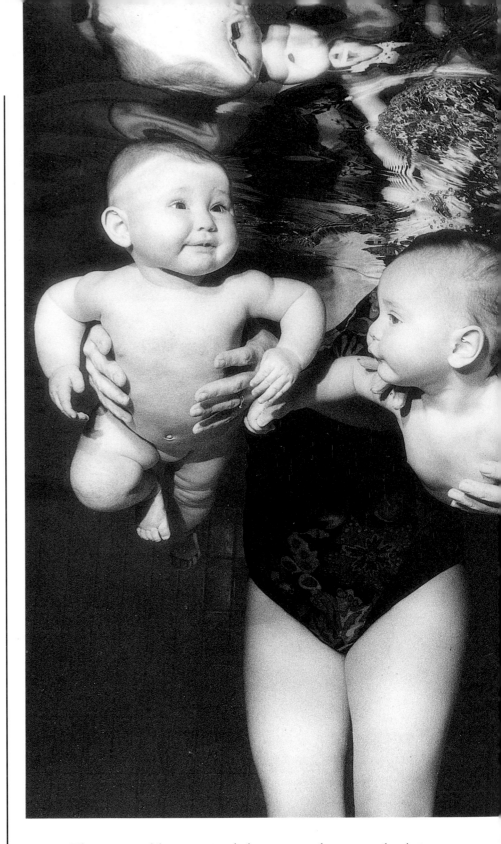

'   The first swimming class Ben went to (at 6 weeks) was a foundation class to teach the babies a series of commands: 'Ready, splash' as they were lifted from the side of the pool to 'splash' the water, and 'Ready, go' in a firm tone as water was gently poured over their head and face. This was followed by a couple of holding positions with a 'Kick, kick, kick, kick' command that at first clearly meant nothing to him. It was pure coincidence if he actually kicked! However, Lauren told us to keep up the word commands in the bath and literally teach them 'kicking' every day.

The other key point about the swimming was that, as Lauren pointed out, we were not aiming to create Olympic swimmers for ambitious mothers to be proud of. The purpose was for the baby to understand and respect the nature of water and to rescue itself in the event of falling in. This involves stimulating their natural breath-holding reflex, preferably before they lose it, and not allowing them time to acquire fear.   '

joints. They were able to control their vertical position both in sitting and in supported standing, earlier than the babies in the control group. However, the same babies were behind in developing movements in a horizontal position. On reaching the crawling stage, there were no observable differences between the two groups. The babies in the experimental group were ahead in all the criteria where muscle strength was necessary. Interestingly, the babies participating in the small Finnish study and those participating in the large German study previously mentioned did not start their aquatic activities before the third month. As already noted by Dr McGraw in Chapter 1, this is late, as it is already the end of the phase when archaic instincts allow adaptation to immersion. It would be interesting to compare children who

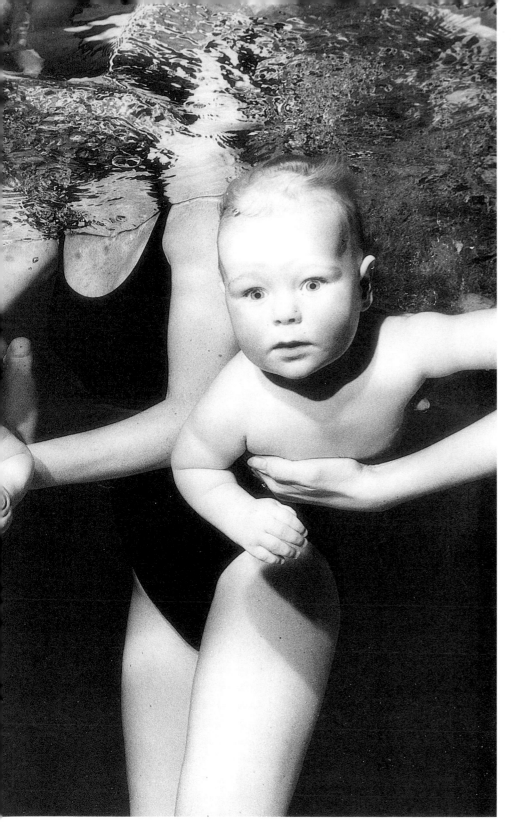

'The second and third swimming lessons included going under water. This involved me learning how to receive Ben gently from Lauren, how to avoid panicking him, and how to dispel any anxiety on his part. He was clearly surprised by the first submersion and spluttered a little, but he never cried or seemed troubled by it.

The difference in him after these three lessons is remarkable. He now seems to realize what 'kick' means when he lies on his front in the pool (on my hands) and I gently sway him through the water as I walk backwards. His underwater swims are also quite different. He doesn't go stiff and straight for the brief seconds below the surface. Even though it is only moments, I can feel how relaxed and at ease his body is. He paddles like mad, kicking strenuously, eyes wide open, as he works his way almost confidently to the surface.

Ben is only 10 weeks at the time of writing, but already — after a total of eight sessions in the water — shows such marked improvement in coordination and confidence that it really is remarkable. I guess it's 'little and often', together with consistent commands, that gradually take effect. He sleeps beautifully after we've been swimming and seems very strong and hungry to learn. As he begins to chuckle instead of just smiling, his pleasure becomes more and more obvious.'

cultivate their aquatic capacities from birth with children who started 'late', i.e. at the age of 3 months.

It must be stressed that the primary objective of these different studies has been to explore the potential benefits of early aquatic activities for human beings and they have provided many answers to questions regarding the child's overall development. They also suggest the need for much more research into an area we are only beginning to understand. Neither of these studies were conducted by medical practitioners. Professor Liselott Diem in Germany is an authority in physical education, while Numminem Pirkko from Finland has a doctorate in sports sciences from the University of Jyväskylä, and also holds a law degree.

So, what does the medical profession think?

4 | Babies and Doctors

There are two kinds of medical doctors: those who have experience of water babies, and those who have not. Dr Ilona Autti-Rämö, from Kaunianinen in Finland, is the best example I know of a practising doctor who is also a practising swimming instructor for babies. Her objective has been to evaluate at which point aquatic activities might help babies and children with disabilities. Her experience leads her to divide disabled babies in to three groups: in the first group she includes all those who can be trained in the same way as healthy babies, but who progress more slowly (Down's syndrome, blindness, spina bifida, muscle diseases, osteogenesis imperfecta, anomalies of the extremities, motor retardation). The babies in the second group are those who are not allowed to dive, but can otherwise follow the method for healthy babies (heart diseases and heart abnormalities, hydrocephalus, etc.) In the third group are all the babies who are allowed to swim if their physiotherapist can regularly teach the parents how to handle the individual needs of their child in water (cerebral palsy, different sorts of hypotonia, etc.). Dr Autti-Rämö is always anxious to have the agreement of the family doctor before the aquatic activities begin.

The basic recommendation of Dr Autti-Rämö is that one should focus on abilities rather than disabilities. She prefers 'integrated swimming groups' comprising both healthy and disabled infants. It must be noted, however, that the role of the instructor is more important if the child is disabled, as the parents need more individual advice.

It has become clear that introducing disabled children to swimming from early infancy can be a very important way to support their psychomotor development and to improve the bonding between them and their parents. In fact, the conclusions of this Finnish doctor, who has daily personal experience of aquatic babies, are that there are only benefits.

As for doctors who have no experience of swimming babies — the vast majority of the medical profession — they tend to disregard the benefits which have been documented and to talk and write about the phenomenon only in terms of risk. A statement published by the American Academy of Pediatrics is typical. The introductory paragraph focuses on diseases: 'giardiasis transmission' and 'water intoxication with seizures'. The first recommendation is a warning: 'a parent who enrols an infant in a water-adjustment program should understand and accept the risks'. The next four recommendations are about 'how to reduce the risks'. The last recommendation reads: 'studies of the frequency of risks to infants from water-adjustment programs should be carried

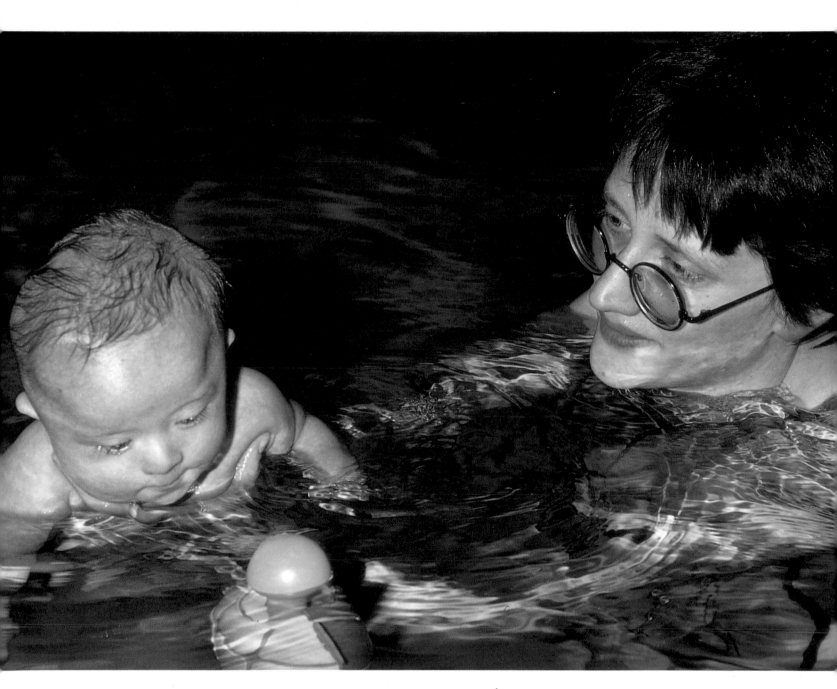

out as soon as possible'. In any other field of medicine it is usual to evaluate both 'risks and benefits' comparatively ... but not, apparently, where water is concerned.

The California Medical Association recently published a fact sheet for general practitioners and family doctors entitled 'Risks of Toddler Swimming Programs'. This fact sheet, designed to help physicians respond to questions about toddler swimming programmes, is just a catalogue of frightening possibilities,

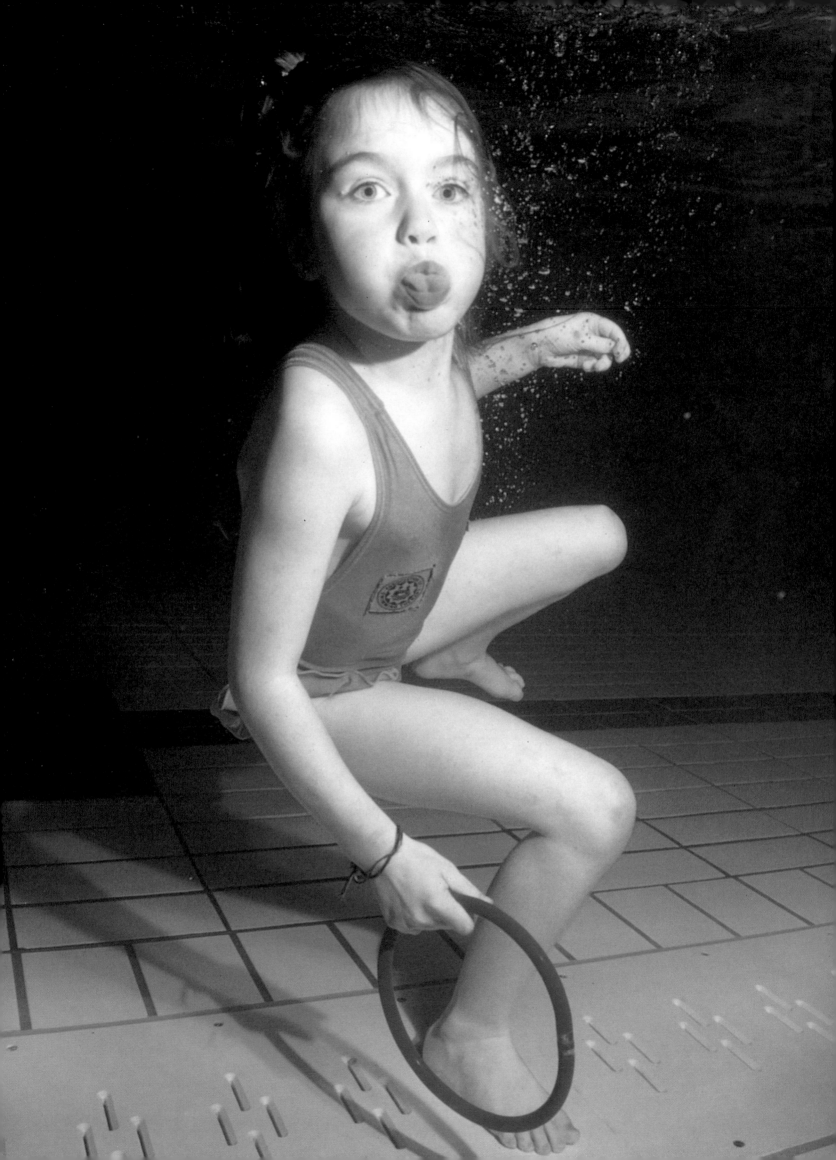

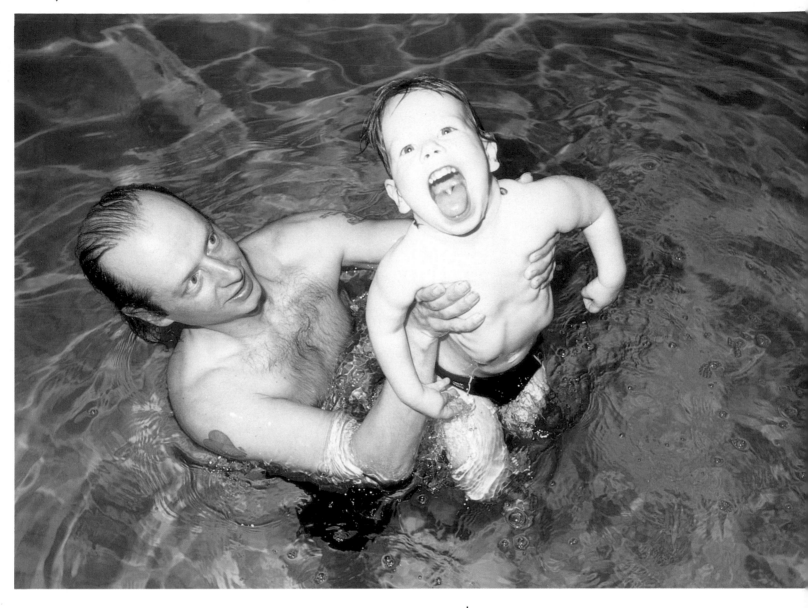

including the danger of instant death. But what are the facts?

GIARDIASIS is a benign disease caused by a protozoa in the small intestine. It occurs throughout the world, particularly among children. Commonly transmitted through food contamination, the main symptoms are diarrhoea, discomfort in the abdomen and loose, pale motions. It responds well to oral treatment. Over the last decade there has been only one report of such an infection in a swimming class, reported in 1984 in the *American Journal of Public Health*.

WATER INTOXICATION is a well-known condition. It is the result of excessive water intake and can be the result of improper feeding practices, of vigorous hydration during a febrile illness, or of administration of tap-water enemas. Water intoxication can cause the level of sodium in the blood to decrease dramatically. The symptoms include restlessness, weakness, vomiting, too much or too little urine, muscle twitching and seizures. The treatment is salt administration and water restriction. A report of water intoxication from swimming appeared in the *Journal of Pediatrics* in 1982, and two reports appeared in *Pediatrics* in 1982 and 1983. In these different cases the children were more than 4 months old and the water intoxication was the consequence of obvious

ABOVE: *Zac, who has cerebral palsy, clearly enjoys the freedom the water gives him. Many doctors who have little or no experience of swimming babies and infants worry that parents who introduce their children to water activities may be exposing them to the risk of water-borne infections. However, the facts show that such infections are very rare.*

LEFT: *A young girl dives down and retrieves a hoop.*

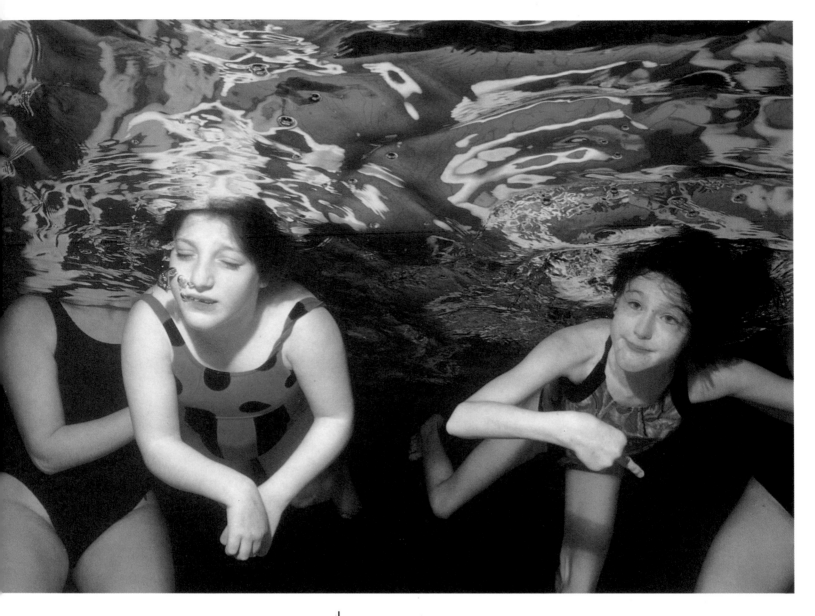

ABOVE: *Two girls swim in and under the water with the guidance of instructors and helpers at the Kensington Emperors, a club devoted to swimming activities for children and adults with mixed abilities and different levels of disabilities.*

RIGHT: *A vibrant, healthy young infant, who has been attending baby swimming classes since he was a few months old, shows remarkable aquatic skills at 11 months. However, many infants of a similar age may never even have been to a pool.*

mistakes. In the 1983 case published in *Pediatrics*, for example, the 11-month-old baby girl had a 60-minute swimming lesson. It is difficult to imagine that such accidents can happen with experienced swimming instructors who specialize in babies.

EAR INFECTION is another cause of concern for some doctors. If the eardrum is intact, however, there is no reason why immersion might cause ear infection. But what about children with grommets (small tubes inserted in the eardrum to allow the draining of fluid from the middle ear)? All the studies comparing swimmers and non-swimmers with grommets found that the only difference between the two groups was that swimmers were at less risk. The studies also found that earplugs are useless in the prevention of an infection. Dr D. F. Chapman, the author of the first of these series of studies in 1980, wrote that advising children with grommets not to swim 'causes distress, delays the acquisition of a life-saving skill and is based on no published evidence'.

In 1992 a doctor from the Royal National Throat Nose and Ear Hospital in London could write in the *British Medical Journal* that 'twelve years and numerous studies later, this statement remains true'. Fortunately, not all doctors consistently adopt the role of killjoy.

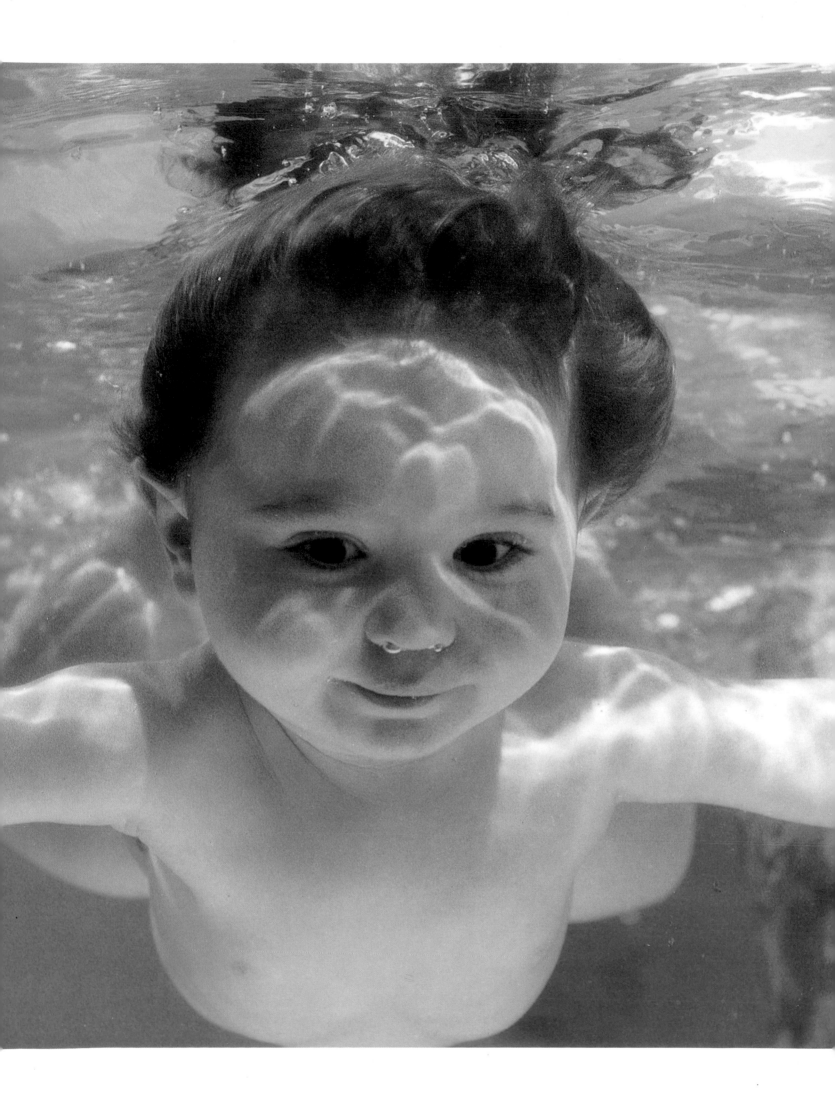

5 | Pregnancy

Considering myself to be a semi-aquatic human being, I was particularly attracted to the water during my pregnancy. The moment I entered the pool area I felt relaxed, the water felt good and my heavy, tired frame was at last relatively weightless. My breathing became regular and I wallowed in the sheer pleasure of swimming and feeling that I was also relieving the gravitational force on the babies that I was carrying within me. ’

Within the uterus the fetus floats in clear, watery fluid, the composition of which is very similar to sea water.

Fetuses are water babies. At term the baby is submerged in about 1 litre (2 pints) of clear, watery fluid. This amniotic fluid protects the baby from direct injury, helps maintain its temperature, allows it free movement and permits hormonal fluid and electrolyte exchanges. It is a kind of repository for the baby's secretions and excretions. Its composition is basically no different from that of maternal plasma. In fact, it is very similar to sea water. This fluid comes from several sources. It is partly secreted by the amnion, the membrane of the bag in which the baby floats, and it is added to by the baby's urine. Amniotic fluid is renewed at an incredible speed: more than one third is replaced each hour.

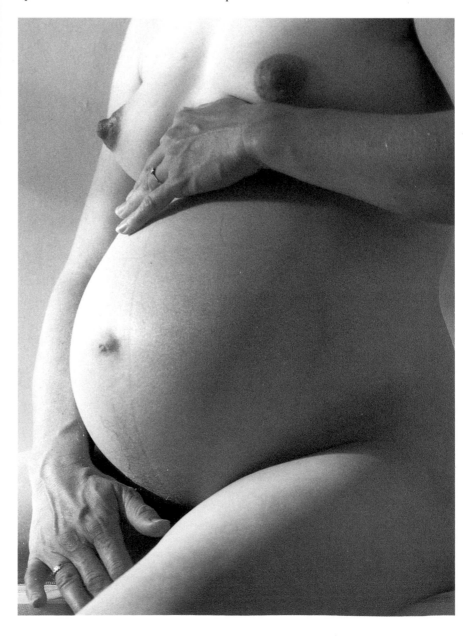

It is mostly during this strictly aquatic phase of human life that the basic adaptive systems reach maturity. In other words, it is mostly during our fetal life that we build our future health. This fact alone should make the well-being of pregnant women a public health priority. In the scientific context of the 1990s we are in a position to explain how the emotional state of a pregnant woman can influence the development of her baby. We know that when a pregnant woman is not happy, when she is not in control of her daily life — for example, when she is constantly dominated by an authoritarian husband — she tends to increase her level of different stress hormones, particularly 'cortisol', which is released by the adrenal gland. Cortisol acts as an inhibitor of fetal growth. Of course, the placenta has the capacity to protect the baby against too much cortisol, but this system of protection has its limits.

In any society other than ours, the extended family, consisting of grandparents, parents, children and grandchildren in close proximity, ensures the protection and well-being of the pregnant woman. In Western society this arrangement has given way to the nuclear family — husband, wife and children often far removed from other relatives. This major social change means that pregnant women no longer have the protection of the community and often have to adapt to their new situation largely unaided. However, even when help is at hand from a woman's mother, there can be problems because their attitudes may be very different. Modern thinking on pregnancy and childbirth has changed significantly from what it used to be 20, or even 10, years ago.

For all these reasons there has been a sudden demand all over the world for what is commonly called 'childbirth education'. The best childbirth educators are those (not necessarily medical professionals) who understand the real needs of modern pregnant women. They know that many young women in our society have never seen a newborn baby, so they initiate gatherings where pregnant women can meet and talk with mothers and babies. The sense of community can be reinforced by group activities, such as singing — our singing sessions in Pithiviers were incredibly popular.

Meeting through swimming is another possible means of group support. I will never forget the evening I spent at the swimming pool of Cookie Herkin, near Melbourne. In a short period of time I saw happy babies only days or weeks old playing in water with their mothers. I also saw pregnant women walking in water, swimming, doing different kinds of exercises, or practising floating relaxation with their partner. All these semi-aquatic human beings were obviously familiar with each other, and happy to chat after getting out of the water. I had the same feeling as at the end

It is both safe and beneficial for women to swim during pregnancy. In the later stages water is especially helpful in relieving some of the weight being carried.

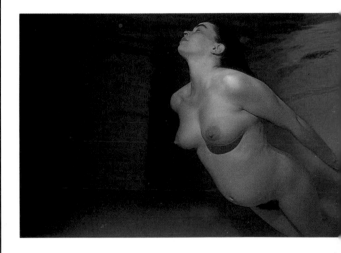

of a singing session in Pithiviers. There was the same sense of community and the same cheerful atmosphere.

There are many Cookie Herkins in the world. They are people who do something to satisfy the needs of pregnant women and make them happier. In fact, they do more for the health of the next generation than any other category of health professionals.

It is unhelpful to be prescriptive about what pregnant women should do while in the water. There are women who cannot swim but feel attracted by water when pregnant. They are happy to walk in water and to do some simple exercises. Others are well-trained swimmers who are happy to swim many lengths. Whatever the case, swimming is probably the only sport that can be practised by pregnant women up to term. The British

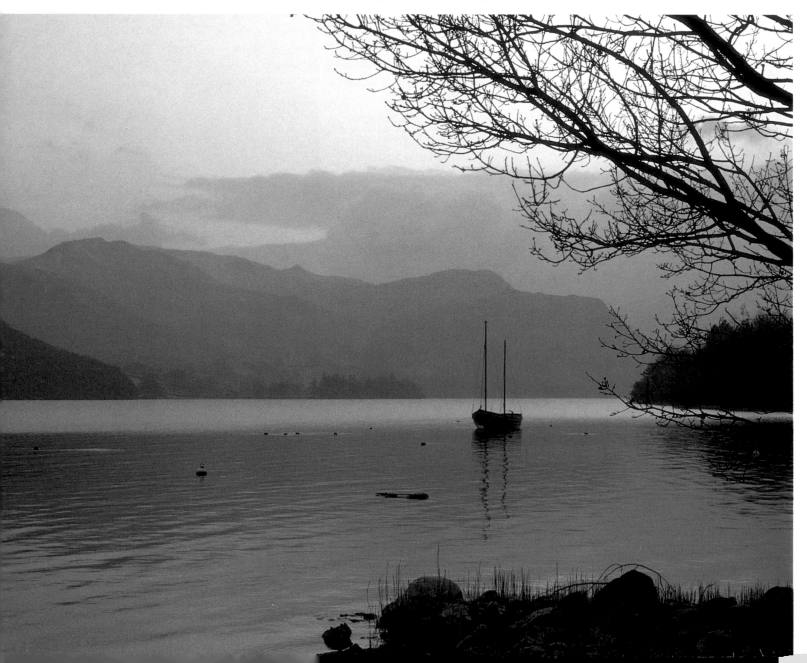

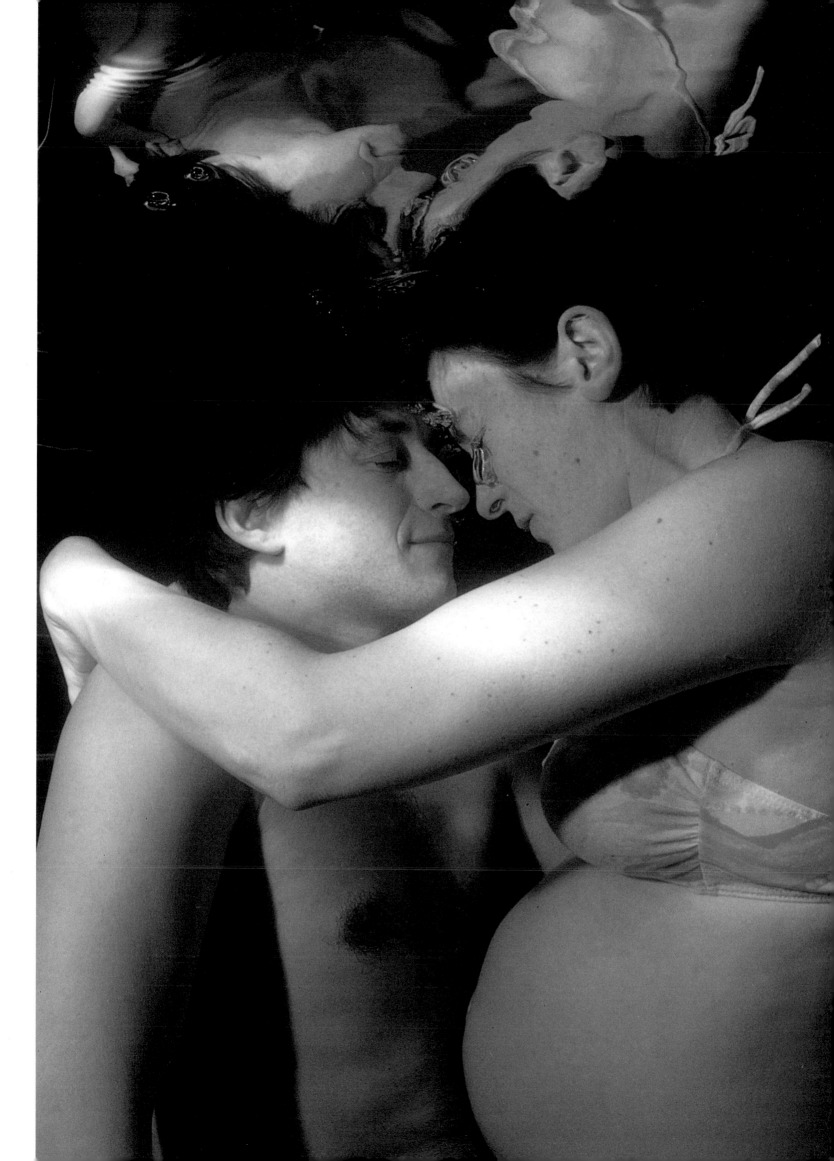

'At weekends I took part in antenatal exercise classes in water. I enjoyed these sessions very much because they relaxed me, while at the same time they increased my physical stamina and helped me to remain supple. I also attended weekly yoga classes for pregnant women, which I found particularly helpful for relaxation and breathing control.

At that time I was suffering from severe heart palpitations and it was through these classes that I managed to control them until they eventually stopped altogether.

I continued the yoga classes right up to the end of my pregnancy, but because I was carrying twins, I was extremely heavy and found it increasingly difficult to keep up with the exercises. Swimming, on the other hand, presented no such difficulty. '

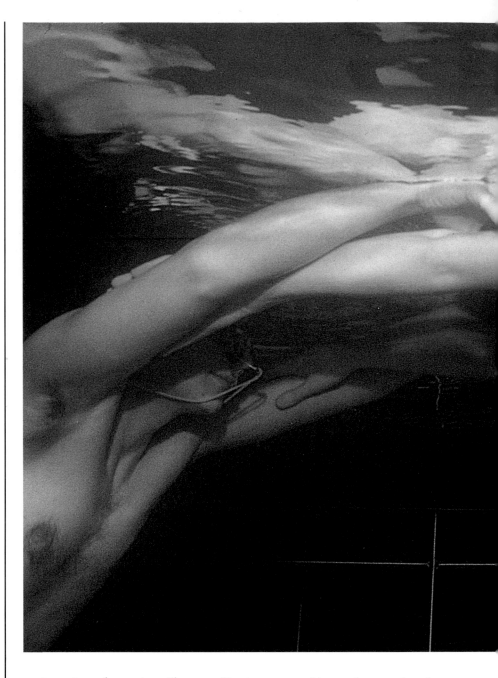

swimming champion Sharron Davies swam $1\frac{1}{2}$ miles on the day she was due to give birth!

When hearing about pregnant women who meet in water, most of us first visualize the public swimming pool round the corner. In fact, before the era of indoor swimming pools, nobody would have thought of swimming sessions for pregnant women. But for some women the image of a municipal pool with its cold tiling is not at all attractive. It does not fit their notion of a natural environment, such as a river, a lake, or a tropical sea. In this situation the imagination has an important part to play. Mundane surroundings can be overcome by thinking of beautiful places and relaxing experiences. While very few pregnant women are lucky enough to swim with dolphins, those who do help to fuel the fantasies of those who can only dream.

Pregnant women all over the world are fascinated by dolphins and their apparent capacity to detect the presence of the baby in the womb. This is attributed to the dolphins' sonar system, which seems to allow them to 'scan' the abdomen of pregnant

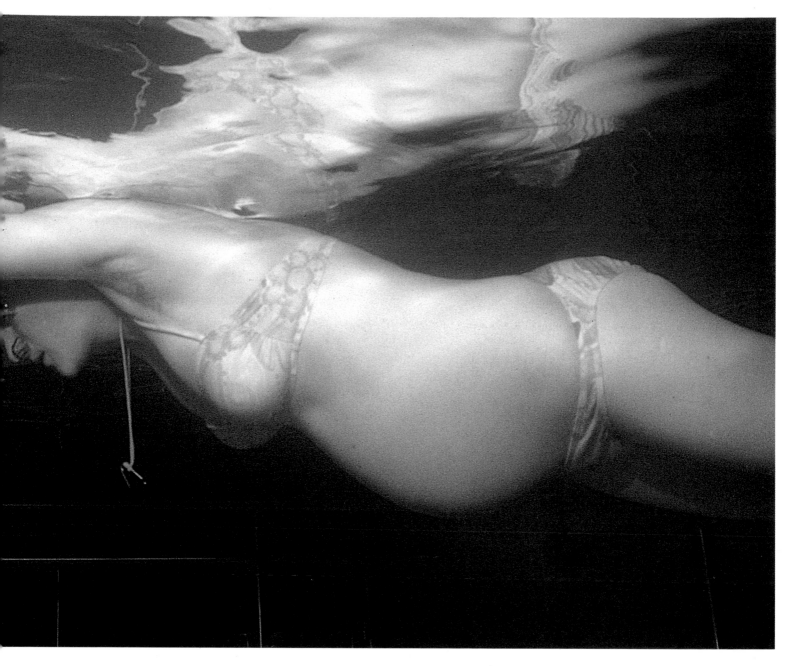

women. Experts in ultrasound do not dismiss this possibility, even though the ultrasound frequencies used by dolphins are counted in tens of kilohertz (tens of thousands of hertz), while the frequencies of ultrasounds used by doctors to see the fetus are counted in megahertz (millions of hertz). The dreams and fantasies induced by such stories are probably as beneficial for the emotional balance of pregnant women as those induced by the sight of a fetus on a screen in an obstetrics department. Women and dolphins have always been linked in the human imagination, as Shakespeare noted in *A Midsummer Night's Dream* :

> 'Since once I sat upon a promontory,
> And heard a mermaid on a dolphin's back...'

Numerous modern statistics confirm the influence of the emotional state of the pregnant woman on the development of her baby in the womb. Two Finnish psychiatrists traced 167 children who were still in the womb when their fathers died during World

An expectant couple practise aqua-natal exercises. These combine yoga techniques with swimming, so they help with breath control and general fitness, thus preparing the woman's body for giving birth.

'Having undertaken yoga and swimming separately I was particularly interested to discover, while on a photographic trip to Ostend in March 1994, a class that combined antenatal swimming and yoga. 'Aquarius', as the class is called, is headed by Isabelle Gabriels and Yves de Smedt. Isabelle had practised yoga during her pregnancy but it was her meeting with Dr Ponette, who specialized in underwater deliveries at the H. Serruys Hospital, that led her to want more from her yoga classes. Through her yoga teacher she heard of a man named René Depelseneer, who had devised yoga classes in water. Isabelle travelled regularly to Brussels with Yves to take part in these sessions before she eventually delivered her son, Ilja, in water, under Dr Ponette's supervision.

It could be said that Ilja's birth was the real inspiration behind 'Aquarius', for it was not long after his arrival that Isabelle trained to teach Depelseneer's techniques and also learned to teach babies to swim. Her plan was to bring the two disciplines together in Ostend so that couples could experience the benefits of water during pregnancy and birth, and then experience the joys of swimming with their infants.'

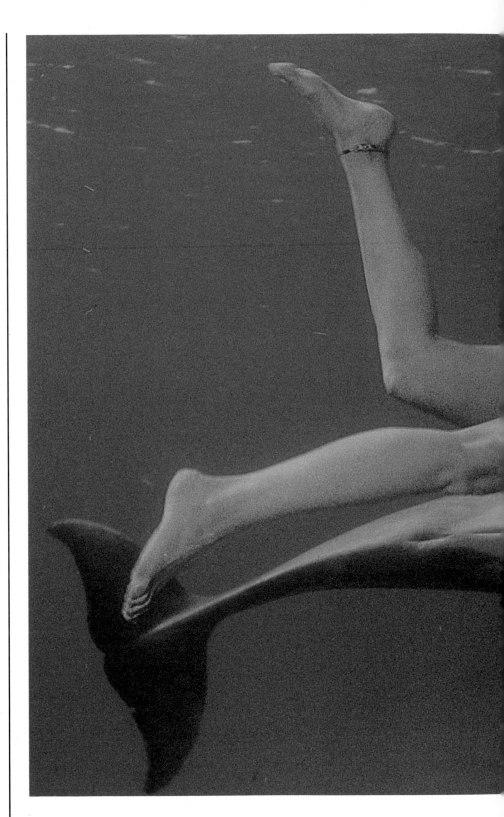

War II, and they also traced 168 children whose fathers died during the first year following the birth. All these children were monitored for 35 years. Only those who were still in the womb at the time of the bereavement were at high risk of mental disorders, alcoholism or criminality. This study suggests that the emotional state of the pregnant woman has more long-term effect on the baby than the emotional state of the mother just after the birth.

Recently we have seen an explosion of different studies demonstrating that babies who had difficulty growing in the womb are at risk from all sorts of adult diseases. For example, a baby whose birth weight is low compared with the weight of its

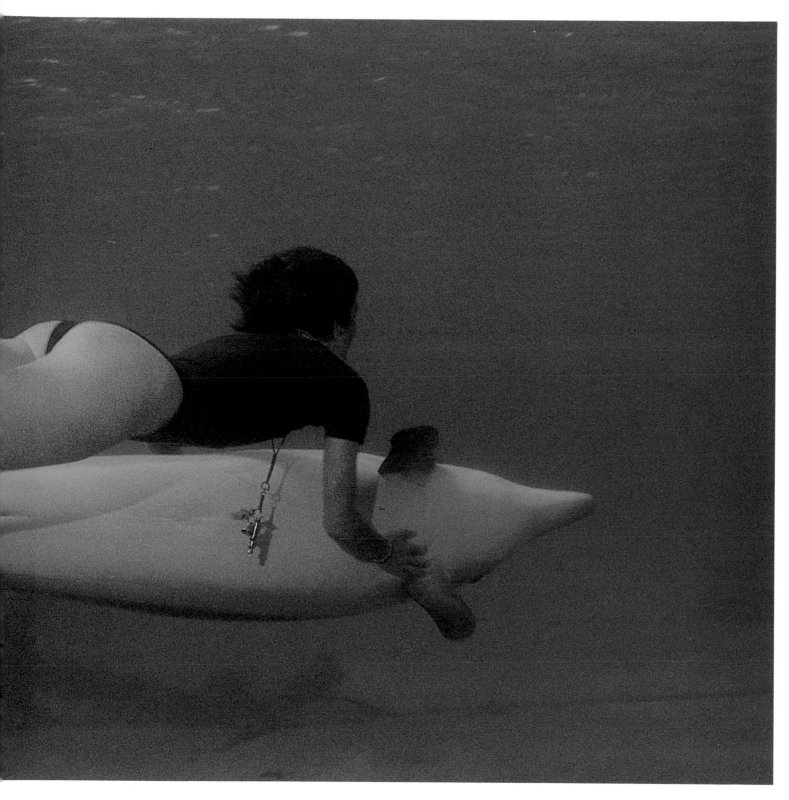

placenta is at risk of heart disease 50 or 60 years later; a baby born with a small abdominal circumference (indicating growing difficulties during the last trimester of fetal life, when the liver is supposed to develop dramatically) is at risk of high cholesterol levels when an adult. In the UK the blood pressure of thousands of children and adults was evaluated. At all ages beyond infancy those who weighed less at birth were more likely to have high blood pressure, and the tendency increases with age.

A Danish team has found that women experiencing unexplained recurrent miscarriages had, on average, a lower than normal birthweight themselves. Similarly, comparison between

Dolphins are particularly interesting to pregnant women because of their apparent capacity to detect the presence of the baby in the womb.

'Isabelle's sessions are held in a hydrotherapy pool filled with diluted sea water filtered through pipes. The water is always deliciously warm and never clings to the skin in the way chlorinated water does.

Over time Isabelle has developed her own techniques. She encourages the male partners to attend the sessions so that they learn to care for their wife's emotional and physical needs during labour.

Exercises consist of long, slow breathing sessions, where couples completely submerge under water, gently exhaling while holding and looking at each other.

Exercises to overcome fear of water and birth, and which also increase breath control, involve acting out the birth process under water. A line of up to six people stand legs apart, forming an underwater tunnel. Each person takes turns at swimming through the tunnel, once head first and then feet first to simulate the breech position.

The most sensual exercise to watch and photograph involves the man supporting the woman by her legs so that her body stretches out in the water. He then gently propels her around the pool, either face up or down, but always with her head under the surface. Wearing a nose clip, the woman takes a quick mouthful of air before being plunged back into rhythmical ecstasy. I can vouch for this, as Isabelle performed this exercise on me. After 10 minutes I was in another world. Her hold on my body was strong and caring, but never interfered with my feeling of weightlessness and freedom of movement.

Apparently, Dr Ponette always knows when couples delivering under his supervision have attended Isabelle and Yves' aqua-natal classes — it is easy to see why.'

schizophrenics and their siblings established a relationship between mental illness and low birthweight. Furthermore, according to a Swedish study, schizophrenics had an average smaller head circumference than a control group of newborns.

There are many factors that can influence the growth of the baby in the womb. The emotional state of the mother is one of these influences. It is well known that cigarettes, alcohol, drugs and certain urinary and genital infections have a negative effect. Some researchers have also recently claimed that frequent exposure to ultrasounds might be another inhibiting factor in fetal growth. This was first suggested by a study comparing two groups of monkeys. The pregnant monkeys who were not exposed to ultrasounds had simulations of ultrasound scans so that the difference could not be attributed to emotional factors. An Australian study with human beings, involving about 3,000 women, led to the same conclusions.

The growth of the fetus also depends on what the mother eats. While many people in the West consume more than enough proteins and calories, the main difference between the diet of one person and the diet of another is the proportion of different sorts of fat. This century has turned a new page in the history of human nutrition. In nature molecules of so-called unsaturated fatty acids usually have a U shape (*cis*). Since the processing of oils and the introduction of margarines, more and more molecules of unsaturated fatty acids used in human nutrition have a different shape (*trans*). Today these man-made molecules represent between 4 and 12 per cent of the fat consumed. They are abundant in such products as biscuits, cakes, French fries and fast food in general. Our bodies cannot distinguish the *cis* and the *trans* forms of fat at the stages of digestion, intestinal absorption and storage. But the *trans* molecules behave like blocking agents at the level of important metabolic pathways. The important news is that the trans molecules are transmitted from mother to baby through the placenta and that they probably impair the growth of the baby fetus. Newborn babies who have a high level of transfatty acids in their blood have a tendency to be 'small for dates' (i.e. small considering the age of the pregnancy). The practical and financial implications of this discovery are staggering, not least in terms of public health.

There is a tendency to focus on the baby's weight as the main criterion to evaluate nutritional needs during pregnancy. But where human beings are concerned, the main issue should be the development of the brain. Research since 1989 indicates that the growing brain has special needs. It is almost as if the fetal brain has

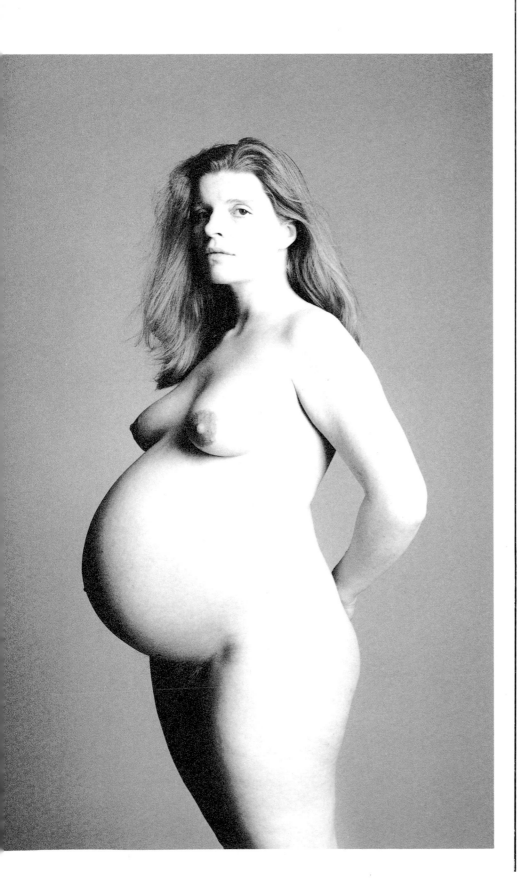

Antenatal care is designed to help women through all aspects of pregnancy, but particular attention is paid to diet.

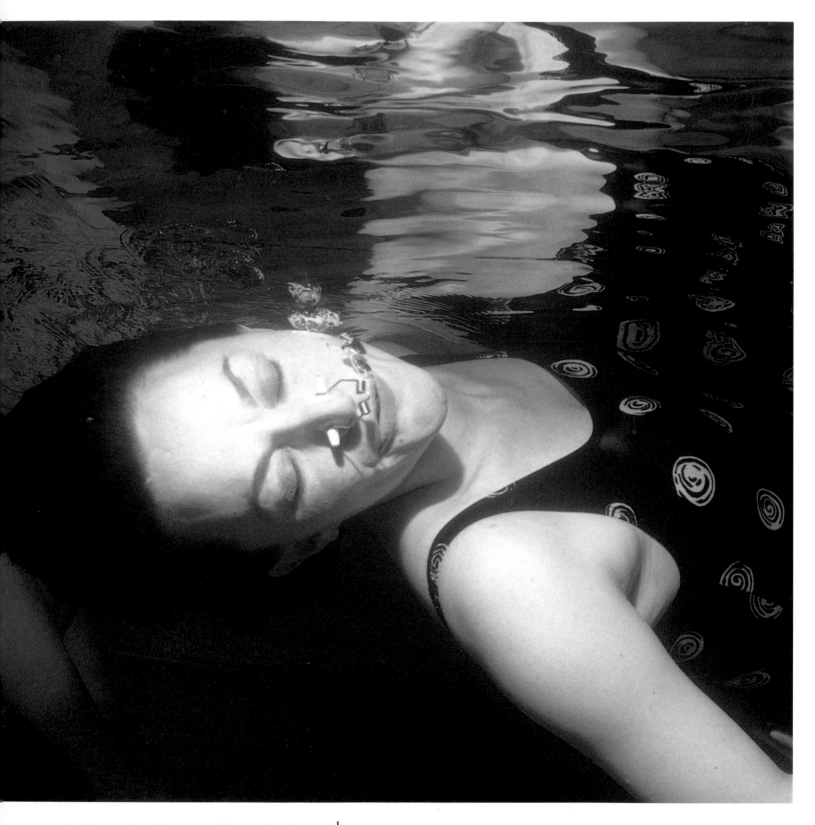

The relaxing effects of water are transmitted to the fetus, whether the mother is submerged in it or simply nearby.

a thirst for a particular family of fatty acids known as long chain omega-three polyunsaturates. These special fatty acids are abundant only in seafood, although the 'parent' of these fatty acids can be found in green plants on land. This molecule has to be transformed in the maternal body before being usable, and this is a complex process which has its own limits.

I am all attention when hearing women claim that their need to eat fish is increased when they are pregnant. This brings us back, in a roundabout way, to the attraction many pregnant women feel towards the sea.

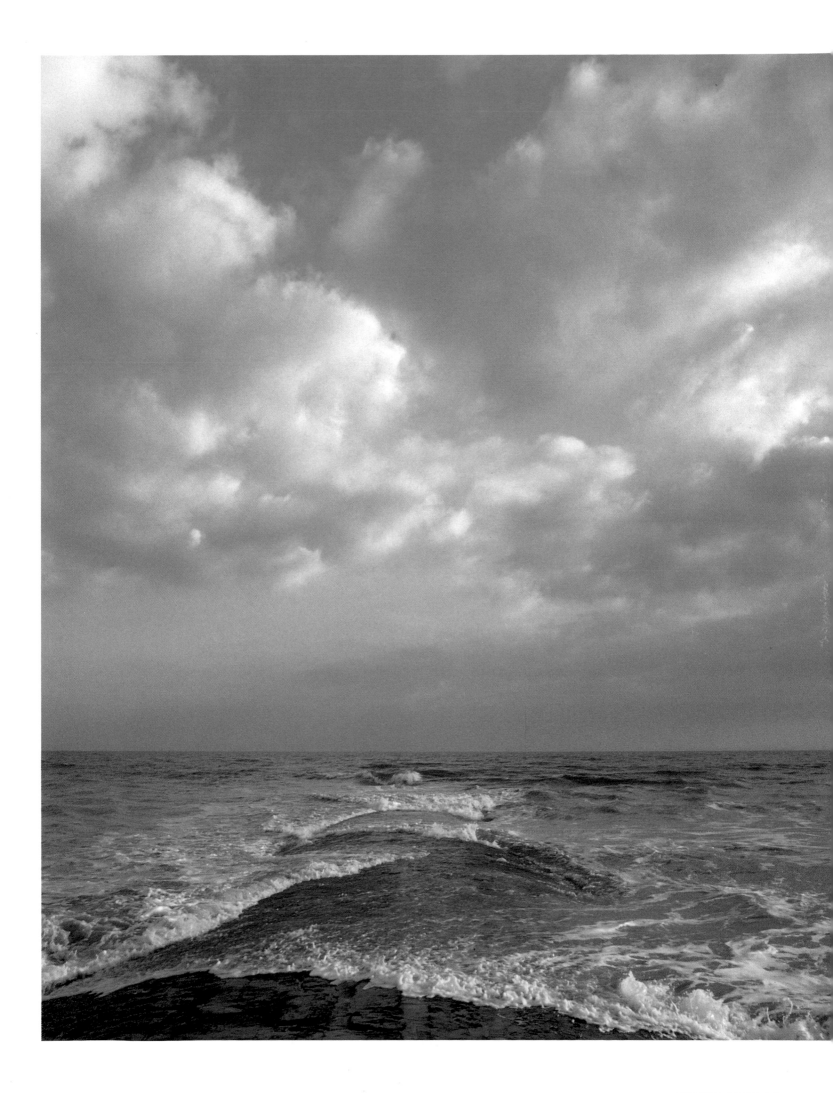

6 | Birth in a Female Environment

' While researching the photographic opportunities I needed to produce this book, I was convinced that to photograph a baby being born under water would be an excellent way to show what actually happens. But how?

I knew of the work being done at the H. Serruys Hospital in Ostend, Belgium, under the pioneering influence of Dr Herman Ponette, who introduced water births there in 1983 after visiting Michel Odent in Pithiviers. Since then he has helped over 1,500 women deliver successfully in water.

I discovered that the women who deliver in water at H. Serruys Hospital do so in a specially designed hydrolized birthing tub made of perspex. '

All over the world, water has always been seen as the ultimate female principle, the Mother of all things. For example, both the letter M, the 'Mother letter', and its inverted form W, are descended from Egyptian ideograms representing water in the form of waves. Is this a key to understanding how water can influence the way human babies are born?

Let's go back to the point I made earlier about many labouring women having an attraction towards water. And let's start from an assumption which is still provocative in some intellectual circles – that human beings have instincts. This is the main lesson we have learned from the swimming behaviour of babies. It is now categorically known that babies, whatever their ethnic origin, can automatically propel themselves under water, but appear to lose this instinctive ability around the age of 4 months. In fact, the primitive brain structures which control automatic behaviours do not vanish – they simply become inhibited, controlled and altered by the gigantic development of our new, rational brain, the neocortex. Human instincts are not burnt-out fires – they keep smouldering.

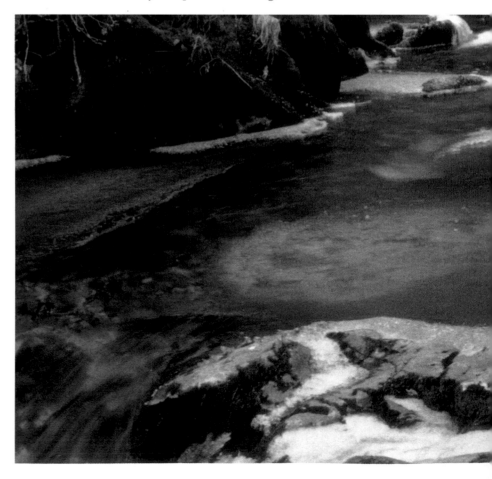

Giving birth is an instinct. This means that when a woman is in labour, the most active part of her body is her primitive brain. Nowadays the primitive brain, which governs instincts, is also considered to be a gland that releases hormones. A woman – or any female mammal – cannot give birth without releasing a certain number of hormones such as oxytocin, endorphins and prolactine. All these hormones are produced directly or indirectly by the primitive brain. Current knowledge also indicates that when there are inhibitions during the birth process, they come from the neocortex. The instinctive nature of giving birth means that the new brain loosens its control and takes a back seat.

By understanding the roles of the two brains we are now in a position to see that if water can make giving birth easier, it is by harmonizing the relationship between the old and the new brain. But the effect of water during labour is better understood if we refer first to observations made by midwives. If these observations are brought together, the conclusion is that each time the neocortex is stimulated, the birth process becomes more difficult. Even simple things such as talking in straightforward terms, to

In the days before modern plumbing, pregnant women sometimes bathed in natural pools and rivers.

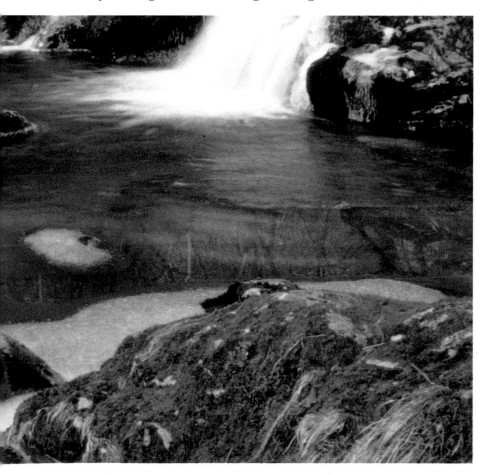

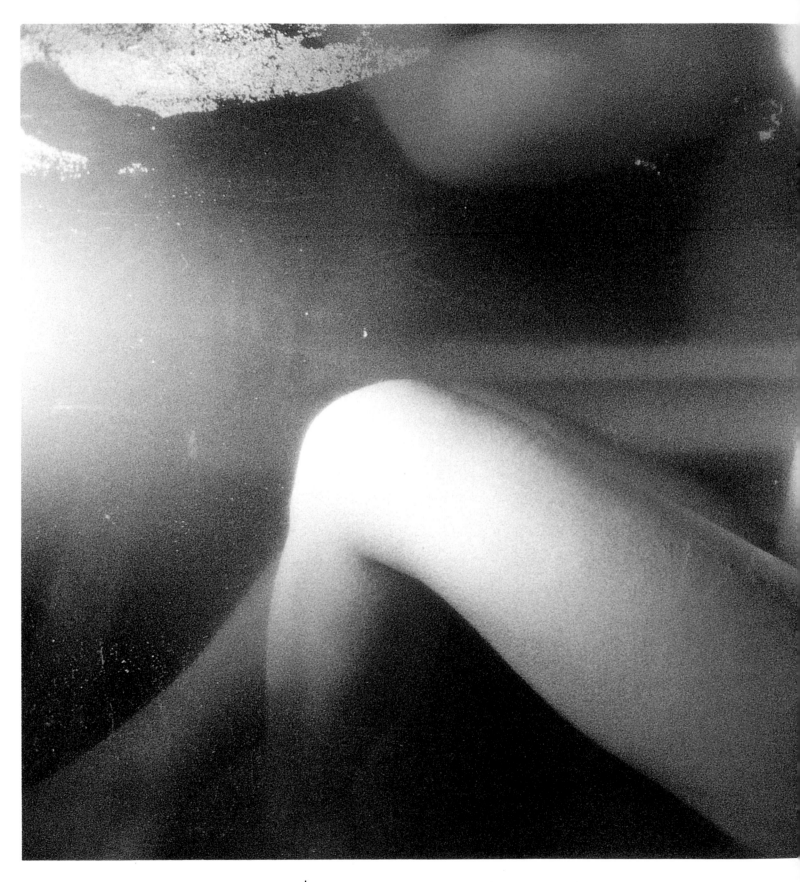

ABOVE: *For centuries many women in labour have had an attraction to water. Water possesses a calming, female quality that can be very reassuring, especially as many modern maternity units are very masculine places.*

reassure, to encourage, or to explain something, or asking such questions as 'What does your husband do?' all stimulate the neocortex. Sensitive midwives don't talk a lot; if they have something to say, they use simple words or body language.

Sight is the most intellectual of our senses, so another way of stimulating the neocortex, and therefore making the birth more difficult, is to keep the labour room brightly lit. Indeed, simply

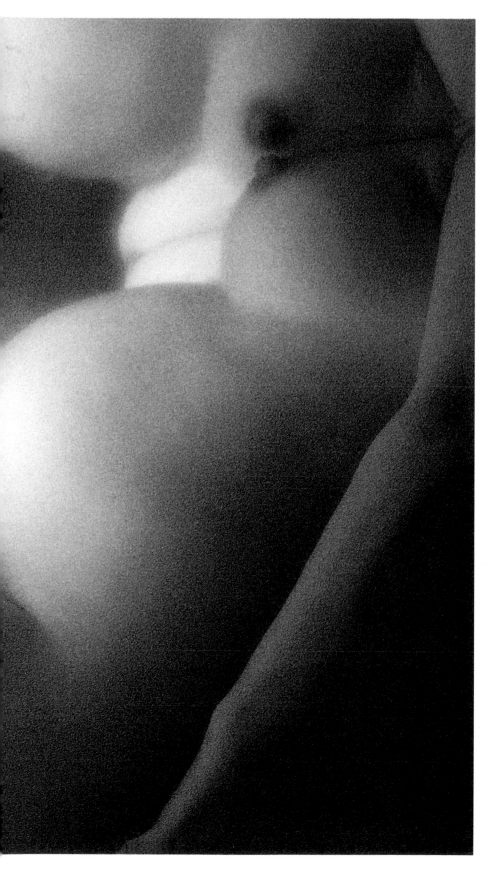

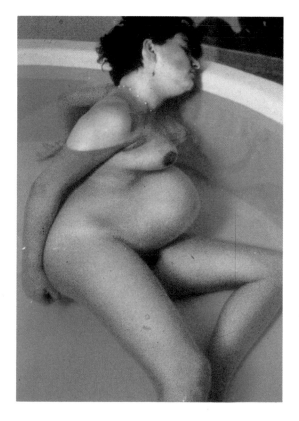

observing the labouring woman will stimulate her neocortex. Remember, you don't feel the same when alone in your bathroom as you do on a stage in front of an audience. Privacy is a basic need during labour, and is common to all mammals. It is ironic that non-human mammals, whose neocortex is not as developed as ours, know better than us what to do to avoid harmful situations. All of them seek privacy. Privacy, the state in which we feel unobserved, is

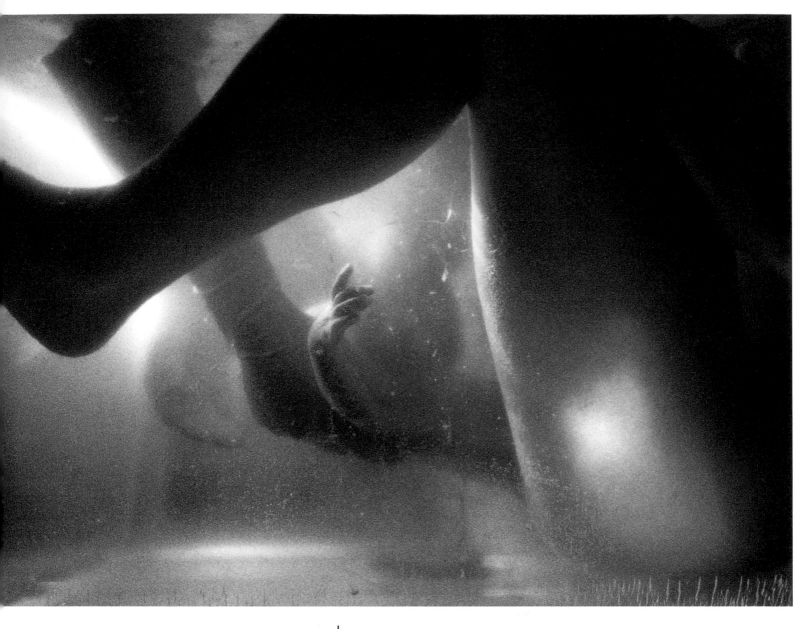

Newborn babies are perfectly adapted to immersion.

' At first sight I found the perspex birthing tub rather gruesome and not as friendly looking as the round blue birthing pools we have in England. However, it looked different when I saw it in action.

It was peaceful and quiet in the room. The lighting was very dim, and soothing music came from a speaker in the wall. I noticed how the bath had lost its harsh appearance, as the expectant mother's body was illuminated by the water. She was comfortable and in control. '

subjective. The main prerequisite to reach this state is to feel secure. Then, our neocortex can more easily take a back seat.

Protection is a fundamental part of midwifery, dating back to the times when women gave birth with only the help of their own mother, or another experienced woman in the extended family. Midwives were originally substitutes for the mother of the one giving birth. This is confirmed by the roots of the word 'midwife', which in many languages means 'mother' or 'grandmother'. Take, for example, the old French 'matrone', the Spanish 'matrona' and the American-English 'granny', all names applied to midwives.

It seems that the kind of privacy labouring women need is compatible with the presence of a mother figure, especially at the stage when they have their bowels open. In fact, some of them openly call out for their 'mummy'.

I recall being present at the birth of a first baby at home. It had been quite straightforward, but afterwards the young mother told me that there came a point when she 'changed gear' and surrendered completely to the experience as her eyes came upon a photo of her mother, who had died some years before. This does not mean that modern women should necessarily give birth with

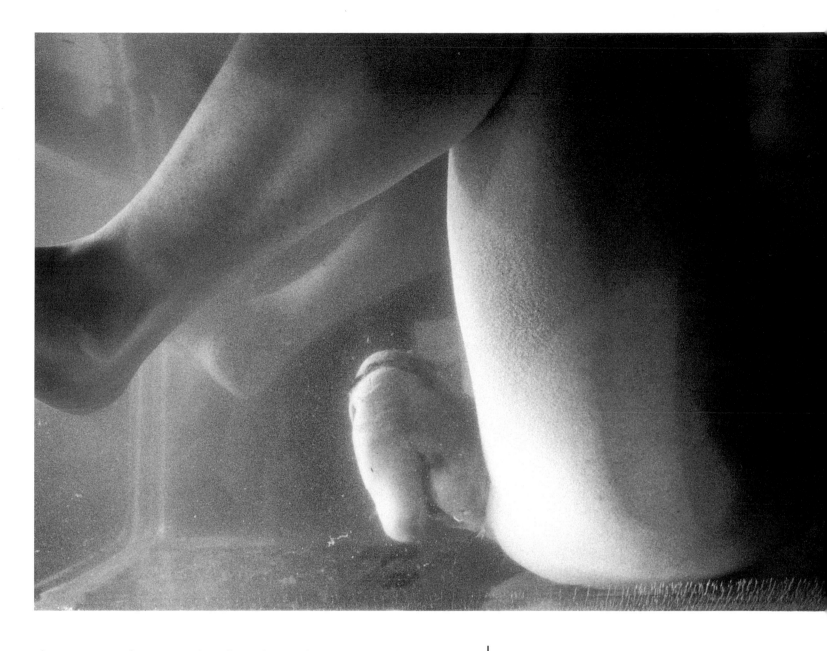

their own mother around. In fact, things change so much between one generation and the next that the older woman's experience may not be relevant to the younger woman. None the less, in some countries, such as Japan, it is still common for a pregnant woman to be close to her mother at the end of the pregnancy.

For various reasons the atmosphere in a typical modern maternity unit is very masculine. This is because many health professionals are men, and high technology is a masculine symbol. In fact, the introduction of electronic heart monitors to the birthing room can be seen as a symptom of a basic ignorance about the birth process. No wonder that the introduction of water can make a difference. Any form of water can work and many midwives have noticed how beneficial a simple shower can be. First of all, it provides privacy, which is a basic requirement of labour. When the labouring woman directs the jet on to her nipples, the uterine contractions can be stimulated via an increased release of the hormone oxytocin. In addition, the sight, smell and sound of water transmit a complex mixture of messages.

The attraction of labouring women to water could not be expressed freely before the age of modern plumbing. However,

A breech baby born under water at H. Serruys Hospital, Ostend. The mother had originally wanted an epidural, but opted for the pain-relieving qualities of water instead.

'Among the births I photographed was a breech birth delivered by Dr Deschacht. The mother had previously requested an epidural, but had finally opted for the bath. Her delivery was incredibly swift and seemed relatively easy and painless. This was rather a surprise to me because I'd believed that many breech births had to be delivered by caesarean section.'

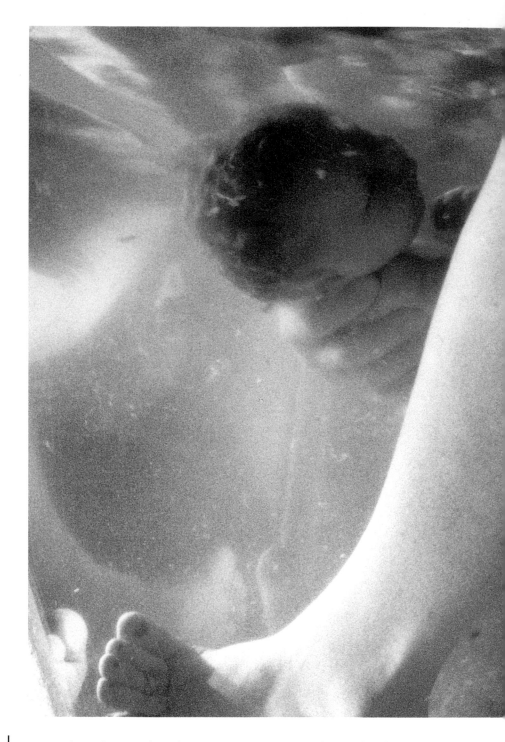

'The first birth I photographed in Ostend was attended by Dr Deschacht. After the new mother had held the baby in her arms for a while, the proud father was allowed to cut the umbilical cord. This is normal practice in Ostend. In fact, if a mother is expecting her second or third child, and her other children are not too young, they are allowed to be present at the birth and can also help to cut the cord.'

water has always played an important part in home births. Husbands could be kept busy for hours boiling water, a practical task intended simply to channel their emotions.

The attraction of water during labour is not new. In certain 'primitive' cultures, such as the Eife Pygmies of Zaire's Ituri Forest, there is little interference with the birthing process, and the birthing place is often close to a river. This is also true of other African tribes, and of the Jackwash who live in the Peruvian part of the Amazonian forest. Some Aborigines on the western coast of Australia first paddle in the sea before giving birth on the beach.

According to a Japanese tradition, women living in certain southern islands used to give birth in the sea. In fact, oral history suggests that the use of water during labour and birth under water were probably known among people as diverse as the ancient Egyptians, the Indians in Panama, some Pacific islanders and, perhaps, the Maoris of New Zealand. Written documents suggest that even before the age of running water, many European women

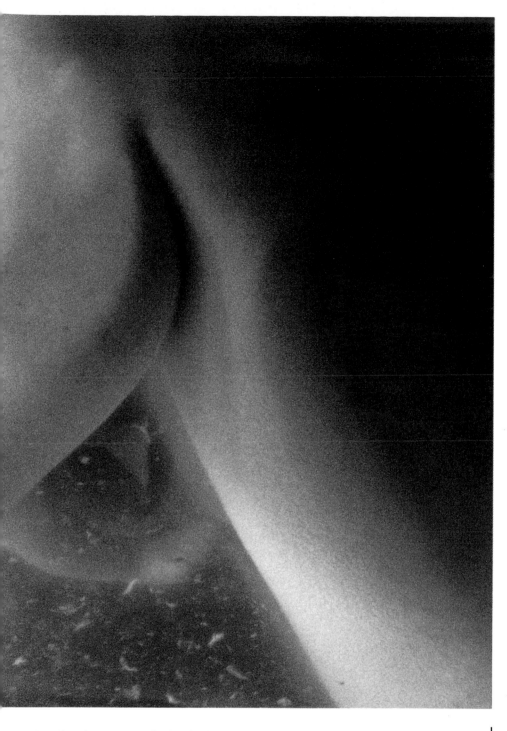

A hand reaches down and gently helps her newborn baby into the world.

took advantage of a bath during labour. The natural pools in the weathered rock of Clach Bhan and Ben Avon in the Cairngorm mountains of Scotland were supposed to have powerful effects on labour pains. In a popular German book published at the beginning of this century, *Die Frau als Hausarzting* (The Woman as Family Doctor), a bath at body temperature followed by a three-minute cooler bath was recommended as being helpful for a difficult labour.

A French medical journal reported an underwater birth as early as 1805. It seems that a pregnant woman did not have time to leave her bath before the baby was born. This means that the use of water during labour was not exceptional in certain parts of France two centuries ago.

Birth and water have also frequently been associated in myths and legends. In ancient Greece Aphrodite, the goddess of love, was born from the foam of the water, while in Cyprus the goddess of love was born on the beach at Paphos.

‘ The second water birth I photographed involved a young woman in her twenties, who was having trouble dealing with the severity of her contractions. She had been in labour a long time, and although the warm water clearly helped, it was hard to watch someone in so much pain, particularly as I had had similar experiences. It was at this time that the midwife came into her own. She remained constantly at the woman's side and kept her going with gently encouraging words.

Dr Ponette then entered the scene, and gently helped ease the child out of its watery environment into the arms of a very tired and relieved young mother. ’

> The H. Serruys maternity unit and the doctors and midwives who work within it have a 'birth without violence' philosophy. From what I witnessed, this is certainly true, and although 'normal' deliveries are frequently undertaken, the staff, when they can, will encourage the gentler option.
>
> It was a wonderful privilege to glimpse into the lives and happenings within a state hospital in a small city. The memory of it will stay with me forever.

> I have always said that I had a low-tech conception with a high-tech delivery. Whereas my dear friend Betty had quite the opposite. Having found it hard to conceive naturally, she had opted for IVF treatment with her partner Hugh, and eventually became pregnant at the age of 44.
>
> Towards the end of her term, she read about the pain-relieving qualities of warm water, and decided at the last minute to order a pool at King's College Hospital, London, where she was due to deliver.
>
> Betty was 5cm dilated when she, Hugh and I arrived at the hospital. The first thing that struck me was how welcoming the delivery room seemed. It had nice curtains and wallpaper, a rocking chair and plants, as well as all the normal accessories associated with delivery rooms.
>
> In the middle of the room was a large, round blue tub. The midwives suggested that Betty undress while they filled it up. It sounded wonderful as the water splashed against the sides. I almost wanted to strip off and get in myself.

As soon as the hospital in which I worked had birthing pools available, some typical scenarios were often repeated. After a certain degree of dilation of the cervix – around the middle of the so-called first stage – some women cannot cope with the intensity of the contractions, so they ask for drugs. This is the time to talk about water. From the first mention of the word, many women forget about drugs and are much more concerned with how long it will take to fill the bath. If they are really impatient, it can help to introduce them right away to the aquatic birthing room. Originally, we used a paddling pool, but this was later replaced by another, deeper pool made of firmer material. Both were blue and round and kept in a small, intimate room which had paintings of dolphins on the light blue walls. It was a restful place in which the mother-to-be could watch and hear the water filling the pool.

As a general rule we advise the woman not to enter the bath before it is full so that we can do a last-minute check on the baby's heart and the temperature of the water. However, when women don't listen to these recommendations, it is a good sign. It means that they have already dramatically reduced their neocortical control and are already on their way 'to another planet'. It is probable that the delivery will be easy and fast. Any 'irrational' behaviour is a positive sign. For example, I have seen women who could not wait and entered the bath while there was still not more than an inch of cool water at the bottom of it. In such a situation the worst thing the midwife can do is to tell the woman off and bring her back to Earth with logical considerations. I have also seen women start to shout and have strong contractions as soon as they saw and heard the running water: they grasped the edge of the pool and the baby was born on the floor before the bath was ready.

However, a majority of women enter the bath when it is full and when the water is at the right temperature – that is, no hotter than body temperature. But between the demand for drugs and the beginning of immersion there is usually a series of very effective contractions and the labour progresses dramatically. As soon as they are in the bath, most women give a great sigh, expressing relief and even well-being. From that time, if the lights have been dimmed, if the baby's father does not behave like an observer, if the midwife keeps a low profile and if there is no camera around, it is probable that the cervix will dilate very quickly.

When the baby is not far away, the contractions can suddenly stop being effective. The mother will feel this and if she trusts what she feels, she just gets out of the water. Leaving the warm water and returning to a cooler atmosphere often triggers off one, two or three irresistible contractions, and the baby is born.

PHOTOGRAPH: Georges Melet

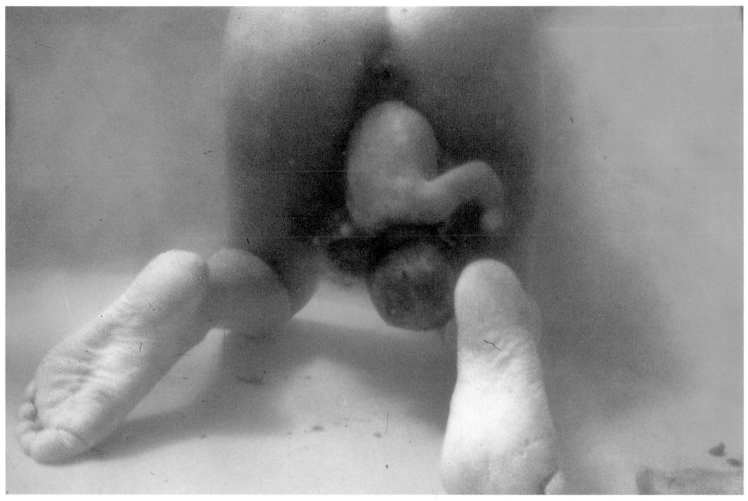

A woman kneeling in the comfort of warm water at Pithiviers Hospital.

'Betty entered the water at about 9 p.m. Her contractions were strong and painful, but it was clear that the warm water helped relieve the discomfort. She was able to move freely within the tub and find the position that was most comfortable for her.

At intervals the midwives would monitor the baby's heartbeat and take Betty's blood pressure. A thermometer hung on the side of the pool; this was regularly checked and the temperature of the water was kept constant.

As Betty's labour progressed and her contractions came closer together, she seemed to slip away from us; she wore headphones and seemed not to want to communicate except to ask for the occasional sip of water or tea.

Calm, peaceful hours passed, the lights were dim, and there was a strong feeling of joyful expectancy in the air. It was hard at times to see Betty in so much pain, but she did seem to cope with it extraordinarily well, and I couldn't help feeling that she and the midwives were in complete control of the situation. A couple of times the midwives asked her if she would like to leave the pool and continue her labour on the bed, but Betty just shook her head. Around five hours after she had first entered the pool, Betty went into the final stages of labour. The midwives at that point came into their own. They persuaded Betty she could do it and helped her control her breathing in between bearing down.

Suddenly through the water a shape could be seen. Betty's excitement was uncontained and with another push Josh came into the world.

It was a joyous moment, Betty had waited so long for this to happen and finally, at 44, had delivered her first child in water and without painkillers.'

Immediately after giving birth, a mother should have nothing else to do than to be with her baby.

Thereafter, the primary concern is the temperature of the room. During the first hour following birth it is rarely too hot for the mother and baby; both share the same needs in terms of temperature. At home it is usual to prepare a portable heater so that warm towels and blankets are available for mother and baby. The second concern is for the privacy of mother and baby. The mother should have nothing else to do than to be with the baby, making eye contact and touching the baby's skin. Any distraction is potentially dangerous, as it may interfere with the release of the hormone oxytocin, which is necessary for the expulsion of the placenta. Such distractions may include cutting the cord before the placenta is expelled, staying in front of the mother, making suggestions about her position, or taking pictures.

No two births are the same. Getting out of the water is certainly most common when the baby's birth is imminent... if the mother trusts what she feels. But there are exceptions: even for a first baby, and typically for subsequent births, the end of the delivery can be very fast in the water. In any birthing place where a pool is available, a birth under water is bound to happen every so often, even if it was not the original aim. When a woman has effective contractions in the pool, it would be counter-productive to repeat vaginal examinations in order to detect the precise time when she should get out of the bath. The risk would be to inhibit the birth process. When a woman feels that she does not have time to leave the water it would be useless to insist.

It is important to know that a birth under water is possible and that a newborn baby is perfectly adapted to immersion. In this case a birth attendant (or the mother herself) has just to catch the baby at the bottom of the pool and to bring him or her gently, in a matter of seconds but without rushing, to the surface. On reaching the cool atmosphere, the baby starts to cry. Then the mother, who is often on her knees, is ready to hold the baby in her arms. The pool should be sufficiently deep so that if the mother is kneeling, the surface of the water is just below her breasts, making skin-to-skin contact and eye-to-eye contact as easy as possible. The first births under water at which I was present happened by surprise. In the hospital at Pithiviers the use of water during labour, and especially births under water, were unplanned and unforeseen.

Before the media began to draw attention to water births, many women gave birth under water without having heard in advance that it was possible. When they reached a certain state of consciousness and had lost their inhibitions, it was as if they knew there were no risks of the baby being drowned. Where does this knowledge come from?

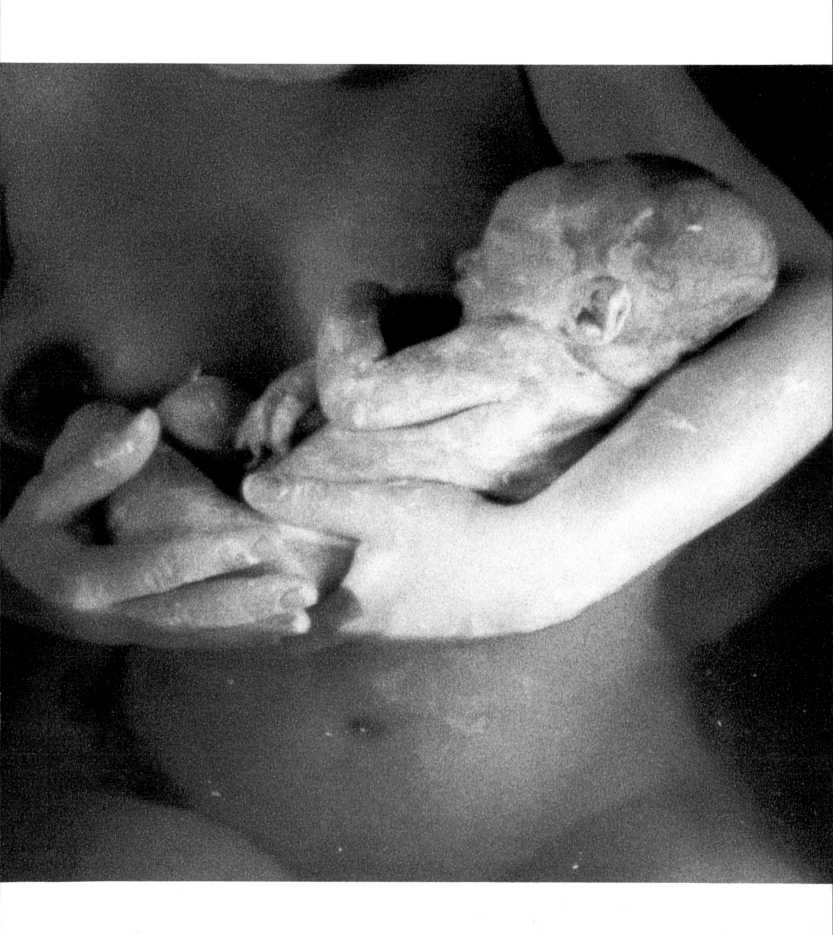

7 | Placebo, Halo and Nocebo

'The use of water during labour requires further research.' This was my only conclusion in a report I published in 1983 in a leading medical journal. Ten years later an article entitled 'Immersion in Water During Labour and/or Birth: the Need for Evaluation' appeared in another journal. In 1994 top researchers, such as a team from the National Perinatal Epidemiology Unit in Oxford, are still in the preliminary stages of tackling this issue. What are the causes of this delay? The main reason is that there are difficulties in assessing the feasibility of such studies. The main obstacles are the so-called placebo, halo and nocebo effects.

Beliefs are powerful factors influencing our state of health. This is arguably the most striking medical discovery of this century, and it certainly complicates the task of those who test the effectiveness of new treatments. They must take into account the powerful PLACEBO EFFECT, whereby faith in a remedy increases its chances of working effectively. The word 'placebo' (from the Latin, meaning 'I shall please') was first used in the 19th century. It referred to dummy treatments that were designed to please the patient. Modern tests, however, show that up to 40 per cent of patients may report improvement when treated with a placebo in such conditions as angina, arthritis, asthma and eczema.

It was only after the mid-1950s, when many powerful new drugs were developed, that scientists started to measure the placebo effect. Today a placebo is more than a medicine given to please. It is recognized as having potential therapeutic effects.

The placebo effect can be difficult to distinguish from the HALO EFFECT. This is the effect that a physician or any other health-care provider can have on a patient during a medical encounter, regardless of the therapy or procedure provided. This means that in some situations the personality of the doctor and the way a drug is prescribed are more important than the drug itself. (A halo was originally a shimmering ring of light above the heads of angels, which symbolized holiness and mystical healing powers.)

The placebo and halo effects are important factors that must be taken into account when testing the efficacy of a new treatment. For this reason, the standard test is a 'prospective double-blind placebo-controlled randomized trial', which means that neither the patient nor the doctor knows which is the dummy medicine or which the active one. In typical trials two groups of patients are established by drawing lots. While this kind of trial can work well with drugs, it is harder to apply to water.

Imagine that you want to evaluate how effective the birthing pool is in treating a difficult first stage of labour. For obvious reasons the study cannot be double blind — but can it be controlled and

Another water baby comes into the world at the H. Serruys Hospital, Ostend. The mother had instinctively opted for the water bath, rather than go through the conventional methods of childbirth.

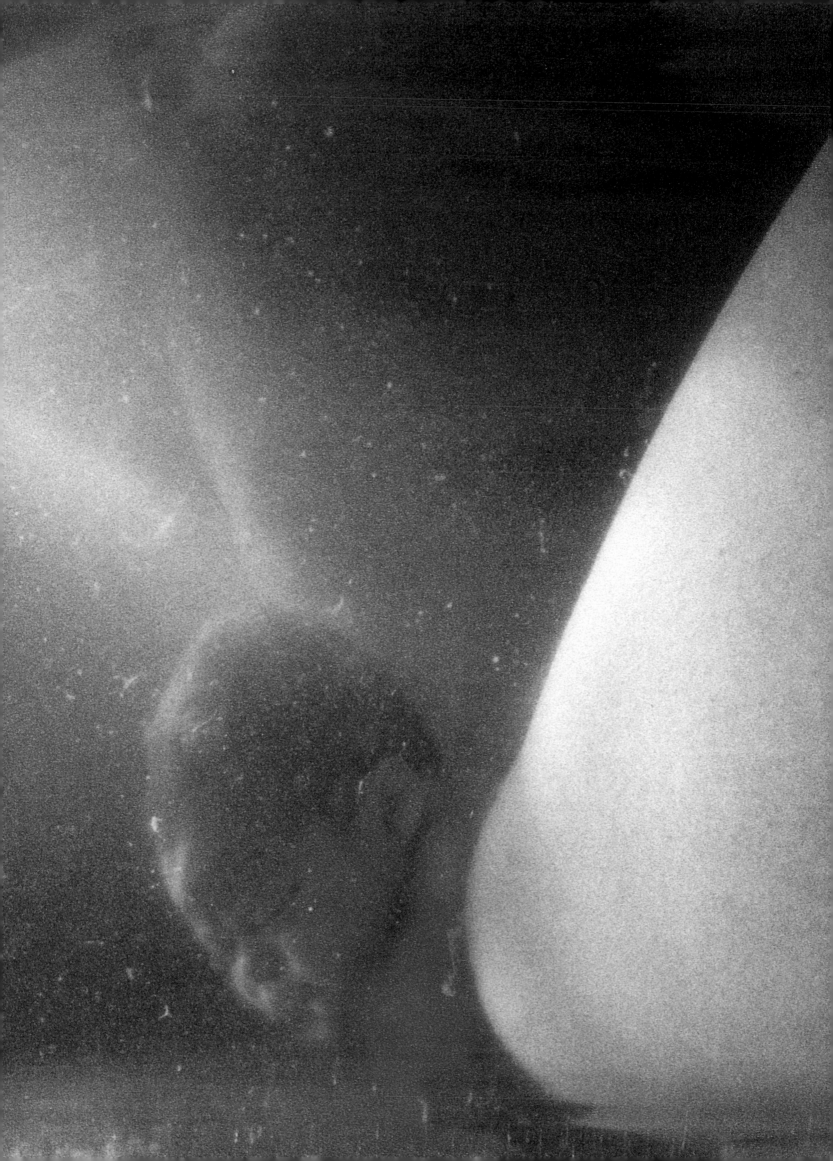

randomized? This is also difficult, as many women would probably refuse to participate in such a study if told that their access to water is to be based on drawing straws. Even if a small group of women agree to participate in the study, what will be measured? The disappointment of those who had not anticipated such an attraction towards water when in labour? The relief of those who have a tendency to say 'leave me alone' when in labour? If the use of water during labour is tested like a treatment, would it be ethical to use a placebo, such as an injection of saline water, as a comparison? How can the same conditions of privacy be guaranteed for both groups? Privacy is subjective and difficult to evaluate.

How to evaluate the effectiveness of a bath on the birth process is a real puzzle for those who know how strong the attraction to water during labour can be and for those who are aware of the importance of privacy during labour. None the less, some kind of research is essential. The first step is to estimate the number of women who have used immersion so that anecdotes reported by the media can be looked at against the statistics. This can be done on a national basis. There are now hundreds of hospitals in the world where birthing pools are available. There are indirect ways to evaluate the effects of a birthing pool. For example, fluctuations in the use of drugs and the rate of intervention in a given hospital can be correlated with the periods when a pool was or was not available. One of the most striking facts associated with the use of birthing pools in Pithiviers hospital was the gradual elimination of drugs and other methods of pain relief. On one occasion when a midwife wanted to administer pethidine, a well-known painkiller, she had to obtain it from the hospital central pharmacy because the maternity unit had ceased to use it!

Before the mid-1970s I often used what I described as 'lumbar reflexotherapy' to relieve the back pains many women experience during labour. This involved stimulating the skin below the lowest rib with intradermic injections (like nettle pricks) of sterile water. It probably worked in the same way as the modern 'TENS' (electric stimulation): the superficial and transitory skin pain competes with the big pain coming from the uterus. The advent of the birthing pool meant that we forgot lumbar reflexotherapy.

Today it would be interesting to compare the drugs bill of different labour suites. The point is to compare immersion against drugs; more precisely, it is to compare their side-effects, as the use of water during labour can be seen as a substitute for drugs. We are at a time in the history of childbirth when we are discovering new reasons to disturb the physiological processes as little as possible. Since the beginning of the 1990s increasing numbers of

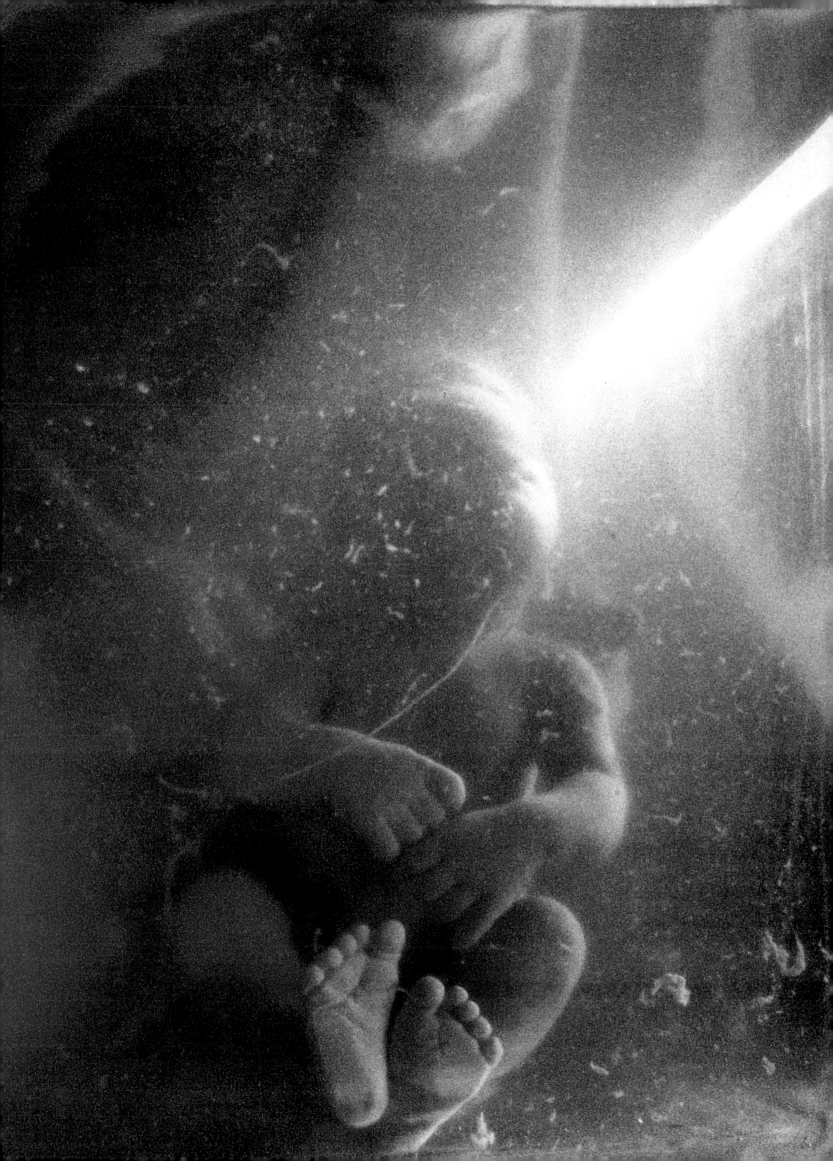

studies have revealed the long-term effects of drugs used during labour. For example, Bertil Jacobson in Sweden studied teenage and adult drug addiction in relation to the treatment given to the mother when she was in labour. His research showed that mothers who used certain drugs when in labour were more likely to have children who became drug addicted. It seems that the potential for drug addiction can start at birth.

There have also been numerous studies demonstrating the side-effects of epidurals. In fact, it is with epidurals that the use of water during labour should be compared, as epidurals and birthing pools nowadays compete. It would be useful to know how many women might forget their demand for an epidural if a birthing pool were offered at the right time by a midwife who feels comfortable with water. It is now well known that epidurals increase the need for drugs to stimulate the contractions, as well as increasing the number of forceps and caesarean deliveries. We can even understand why an epidural can, by itself, be a cause for fetal distress. During a prolonged epidural analgesia the temperature of mother and baby tends to increase, the baby's being usually about 1°C higher than the mother's. According to a British study, 5 per cent of babies can reach a temperature higher than 40°C during an epidural. This is a cause of concern because the fetus has a problem with heat elimination. When its temperature is high, the fetus needs more oxygen, so it is therefore more vulnerable. In fact, such a high fetal temperature can also occur when the mother is immersed in a bath that is too hot. This was probably what happened in the well-publicized water-birth accidents in Bristol. In fact, in one case the water temperature was 39.7°C when the mother entered the pool. In Pithiviers I used to check that the water temperature matched the normal maternal temperature.

Today we are also aware of the increased risk of chronic back pain among mothers who have an epidural. According to studies in Birmingham and London, these back pains are postural, arising from awkward positions. It is easy to see that an epidural, while masking the pains of labour, also masks the pain of poor posture. It is unlikely that relaxing in warm water would have the same effect. (Incidentally, the best treatments I know for postural back pains are prolonged and repeated deep, warm baths.) Another possible long-term side-effect of an epidural might be the increased risk of stress incontinence. According to a Danish study, 27 per cent of women have stress incontinence three months after the birth of their first baby versus 13 per cent among those who had no epidural. After a year it is 7 per cent versus 3 per cent. This is a significant difference, but the report merely concludes: 'epidurals do not protect [against stress incontinence]...'

As far as water is concerned, possible avenues of research are endless. An evaluation might be done among women who have used the birthing pool during labour, and it might be useful to compare say, round, blue birthing pools versus white rectangular ones, or pools made of transparent material. There is no doubt that such studies will be published in the near future. They should counterbalance the NOCEBO EFFECT (from the Latin, meaning 'I shall do harm'), which is when a doctor or anybody else does more harm than good by interfering with someone's beliefs. It is the opposite of the placebo effect, and was originally used when patients in a clinical trial thought they were not receiving the active therapy and were therefore under the effect of negative suggestibility. But it can be understood in a broader way. Although there have been few evaluations of the nocebo effect published in authoritative medical literature, a significant one was conducted recently in the USA. This study compared the deaths of 28,000 adult Chinese-Americans with those of many thousands of Caucasian Americans. Traditional Chinese medicine holds that a person's fate is influenced by the year of birth. For example, someone born in 1907 (a fire year) is supposed to be susceptible to heart disease. In this study the researchers used different criteria to measure the strength of commitment to traditional Chinese culture. The conclusion was that Chinese-Americans die younger if they have a combination of disease and birth year which Chinese medicine considers to be ill-fated, and that more years of life are lost by those who are strongly attached to Chinese traditions.

Unfortunately, doctors are not trained to avoid the nocebo effect. This may have deleterious consequences, particularly during pregnancy and childbirth, when women are more emotional and vulnerable. Home birth, for example, is highly influenced by the nocebo effect (except in the Netherlands). When a woman tells her doctor that she would like to have her baby born at home, she is most likely to be questioned about the risks: 'What will you do if...?' or even 'Why do you want to risk your baby's life?'

Another example of the nocebo effect is the diagnosis of 'non-diseases', such as 'gestational diabetes'. While this sounds very serious, it is, in fact, a temporary impaired tolerance to sugar. Advice about it may easily be included in the dietary recommendations that are given to any pregnant woman and in the recommendations regarding non-weight-bearing exercises, such as swimming. The British epidemiologist R. J. Jarrett calls gestational diabetes a 'nonentity', while in the *American Journal of Obstetrics and Gynecology* it has been called 'a diagnosis still

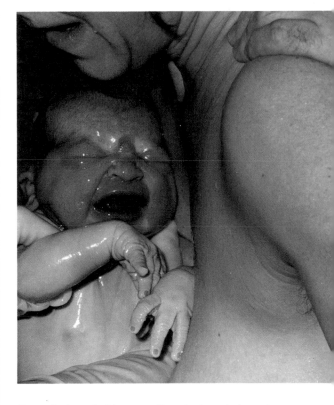

Towards the end of her term, Betty had read about the pain-relieving qualities of water, so ordered a birthing pool at King's College Hospital, where she gave birth.

looking for a disease'. The nocebo effect of the term 'gestational diabetes' has never been properly evaluated, but it is probably high.

As for the use of water during labour, it hovers constantly between the placebo and the nocebo effects, depending on who you talk to. On the one hand, mothers, midwives and even some doctors who have experience of the birthing pool during labour are infectiously enthusiastic about its benefits. On the other hand, those who have no experience of birthing pools tend to talk only of risks. For example, when the use of water during labour is discussed among doctors, their first question is almost always about infection. But those who have extensive experience of birthing pools often forget to mention this topic simply because it is such a rare occurrence. Indeed, recent figures from the large maternity unit of Hillingdon Hospital, west London, reported 418 babies born under water before the end of 1993. Among them, only three went to the special care baby unit for different sorts of infection, which is less than what is expected in a modern obstetrics department.

There are, in fact, theoretical reasons why a baby born under water in a hospital might enjoy greater protection than one born under 'normal' circumstances. We know that a newborn baby is germ-free, but some hours after the birth there will be billions of germs in the gut, mouth, nose and so on. We know also that a human newborn baby has the same levels of antibodies, called IgG, in his/her blood as the mother. In other words, for a newborn baby there are familiar, friendly germs, and there are also unfamiliar and potentially dangerous ones. The question is: which germs will be the first to occupy the territory? The first invaders will be the rulers of the territory. That is why in a hospital, where there is such a diversity of selected microbes, a birth under water can be seen as a guarantee that the baby will meet familiar and friendly germs first. Scaremongering about infection and waterbirth should be looked at in terms of nocebo effect.

Currently, we can only hope that medical training will eventually tackle the placebo, halo and nocebo effects. Many American medical schools seem to be on the right track in educating a new generation of doctors by using role-playing to teach consultation techniques. For example, this may involve a student explaining something to a patient, who is in fact a professional actor or actress. The consultation can be videotaped and replayed to highlight errors.

The use of water during labour might also profit from the work of physiologists. We know, for example, that immersion in warm water has complex biological effects, such as a significant reduction in blood pressure. The levels of such hormones as renin, aldosterone, angiotensine, vasopressin and dopamine have been measured among women who were not in labour. It would be interesting — though difficult — to measure adrenalin levels. This hormone is released when we are faced with threats that require us to fight or flee. When the priority is to save our own person, it is also an advantage to stop or postpone any episode of our sexual life. In other words, we cannot make love if we are threatened by a gun, a cow cannot release milk if she does not feel secure, and a woman has a difficult birth if she is scared or if the room is cold. On the other hand, when a woman has an easy and fast birth it means that her level of adrenalin is low — she is in a state of relaxation, being rather passive and having no tendency to move around. Relaxation and low levels of adrenalin are synonymous, but it is difficult to assess those of a labouring woman in warm water because taking a blood sample will simply make the level rise. While indirect and non-invasive methods might be used in the future, at present we can only assume that immersion in water at a comfortable temperature provides a low level of adrenalin and related hormones. This is one of the more simple physiological explanations we have at our disposal to interpret the apparent positive effect of water immersion during the first stage of labour.

While any progress in our understanding of physiological processes is welcome, perhaps we need to define our terms. The word 'physiological' is used to describe 'normal' bodily functions, but it does not exactly mean normal or that bodily processes should always happen in exactly the same way. It is a kind of reference point from which we cannot deviate too much without the risk of side-effects. Remember, the Greek goddess Nemesis punished man for playing God. We do not want to meet our nemesis by ignoring the physiological reference point. Bodily functions are, to a great extent cross-cultural, and all humans, have to release the same hormones when giving birth.

Every day we are discovering the long-term consequences of deviating from the physiology of birth. Several researchers have established a link between different forms of medically assisted births and the tendency to commit suicide when a teenager. In industrialized countries there has been a dramatic increase of young suicides during these past 10 years. The one exception to this is in the Netherlands — the country where the birth process is disturbed as little as possible.

One cannot interpret the increased number of young suicides without exploring how the capacity to love oneself develops. Indeed, the capacity to love oneself is the basic form of love.

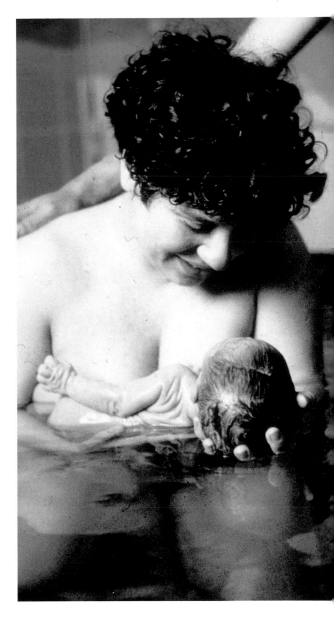

A mother holds her baby after giving birth in water at Pithiviers Hospital, France.

8 | Love, Birth and Water

The links between love, birth and water are gradually conveyed to your subconscious mind as you look at Jessica's beautiful pictures. Look at them again and again, feeling their appeal to your emotions. Words, on the other hand, speak to your intellectual self, and it is my role to make the links clear. That is a difficult task.

In fact, love and birth were allied long before the dawn of the scientific era, but in such a subtle way that we missed the links. If you look at those whose names are associated with love, such as Venus, Buddha and Jesus, the way they were born is presented as a crucial phase of their life. Look, on the other hand, at the beginnings of famous politicians, writers, artists, scientists, musicians, business people and clergymen — their biographies often start with details of their childhood and education. Does this difference mean that birth is a decisive time in the development of the capacity to love?

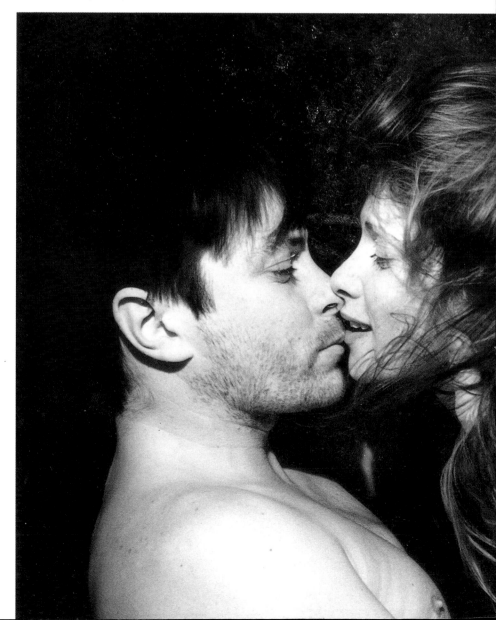

Biology can now suggest answers to this question. Take a baby born a few seconds ago. Because her delivery was as physiological as possible, the mother tends to keep upright, perhaps sitting or kneeling on the floor. She looks at the baby which is still lying between her legs; tentatively she touches it with her fingertips; then more daringly she takes the baby in her arms. Let us look at mother and baby with the eyes of biological scientists.

While mother and baby are close to each other, they have not yet eliminated the hormones they had to release during the birth process. Both of them are in a very special hormonal balance which will last only a short time and never happen again. If we consider the properties of the different hormones involved in the birth process and the time it takes to eliminate them, we will understand that each of these hormones has a specific role to play in the interaction between mother and baby.

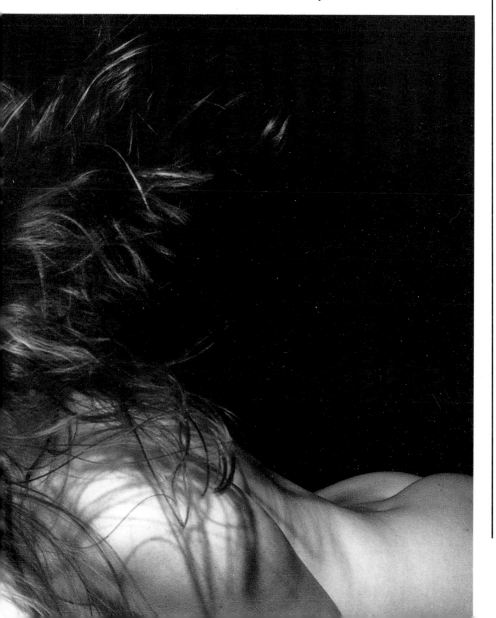

' Certain South African tribeswomen believe that lying down in a shower of rain will germinate their seeds. On the other hand, the Trobriand Islanders of the South Pacific believed that sexual intercourse only prepared a woman's body for conception, and that she actually conceived while bathing in the ocean. The babies that followed were thought to have come from the sacred seaweed that floated in the water.

Many in the Western world might find these stories sentimental, but are they really so strange? Just think of all those Western couples who meet and fall in love while on holiday by the sea, or who do indeed conceive their first child under the influence of sun, sand and water.

In fact, conception usually follows about 12 hours after lovemaking. The DNA strands of the eggs and sperms reach out to touch, and in doing so combine to form a living fetus. Now consider the similarity of the DNA strands to sacred seaweed and the amniotic fluid to the ocean, and these islanders' beliefs no longer seem quite so quaint. '

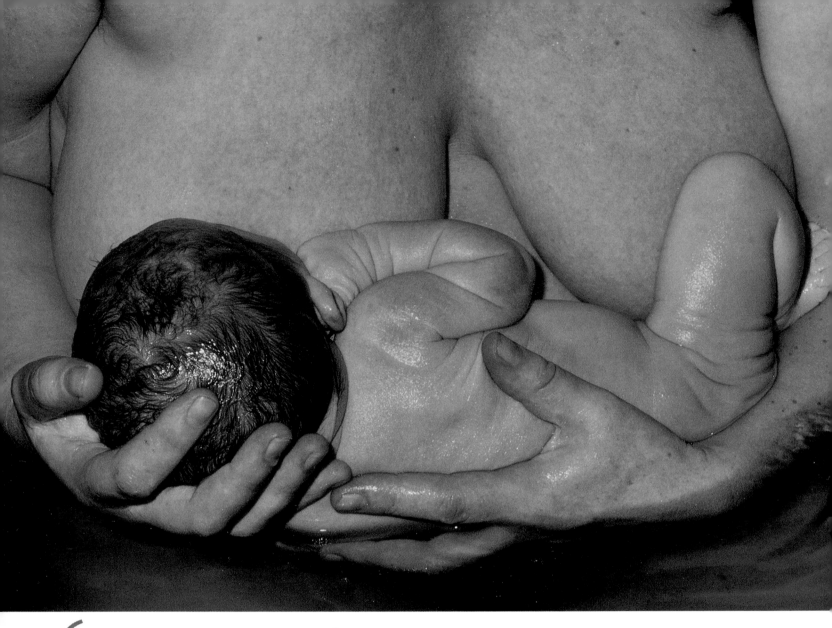

'I have attended several water births and I believe that it is a kind and loving way to have a baby. The women who enter the water always seem to feel instantly more relaxed and at one with themselves – this is also a huge relief for their male partners who often find it distressing to see their loved one in so much pain. Drugs were not used in any of the births I witnessed, so the labouring women were always in control of their bodies and senses, and this is obviously beneficial to both mother and baby. '

ABOVE AND OPPOSITE: *A mother looks at her baby after it has just been born. She takes it in her arms and holds it close to her chest. While mother and baby are close to each other, they are still influenced by the hormones released during the birth process.*

To give birth the mother had to release the hormone oxytocin in order to induce and maintain effective uterine contractions. In fact, it is just after the birth that the level of oxytocin is at its peak. This is important as we know that oxytocin is a hormone that can induce maternal behaviour. (If you inject oxytocin deep into the brain of male rats or virgin female rats and then present them with baby rats, they will behave like mothers.)

It is now clear that during the minutes following birth mother and baby have not yet eliminated the morphine-like hormones that both had to release during the birth process. The main properties of opiates have been known and used for a long time: they create habits and states of dependence. This knowledge therefore suggests that when mother and baby are close to each other during the hour following birth, it is the beginning of a dependence and an attachment.

Hormones belonging to the adrenalin family are also involved in the birth process. The role of adrenalin during labour is complex and there is an obvious rush of it during the very last contractions of an apparently physiological birth – what I call the 'fetus ejection reflex'. At this time women tend to remain upright, need to grasp something or somebody and are full of energy. Other signs of a sudden release of adrenalin include dilated pupils or the need to drink a glass of water, like a speaker in front of an audience. Current knowledge helps us to understand how adrenalin can have a transitory excitatory effect on uterine contractions. It has been demonstrated that at the moment the baby is born the level of maternal adrenalin is high and takes about 15 minutes to return to normal. This is an advantage for the survival of the species, as the mother has enough energy and aggression to protect her newborn baby. If you try to pick up the newborn baby of a female mammal, the mother will react fiercely. She has a strong 'maternal protective aggressive instinct'.

In parallel, the baby has released a large amount of adrenalin-related hormones, and at this point the level can be 15 times higher than normal. The most noticeable effect is that the newborn baby is alert, with big eyes and big pupils. Mothers are fascinated by the eyes of their newborn babies. Mother and baby immediately tend to establish eye-to-eye contact, and this seems to be a very important time in the human mother-baby relationship. It would not be adaptive if mother and baby were sluggish and unaware during the minutes following birth.

Long before our current understanding of the hormonal balance of mother and baby during the hour following birth, scientists observing animal behaviours and studying the process of attachment had already noticed a critical and sensitive period just after birth. This generation of studies started with Konrad Lorenz, who discovered that if he walked very slowly in front of newly hatched goslings, the baby birds followed him about as if he were their mother, and remained attached to him throughout their life. Of course, the existence of a sensitive period among humans cannot be clearly demonstrated: human behaviours tend to amalgamate in the framework of a culture. However, even if the effects are difficult to detect at the level of a particular individual in a given culture, we have enough data to suspect from modern biological sciences that the first hour following birth is probably a vital time in mother-baby attachment. We can also suspect that it is only at the level of civilization that these effects can be recognized.

In the scientific context of the 1990s we should be concerned about the powerful ways in which we can interfere with the hormonal balance of mothers and babies in the period surrounding birth. Each time a drug is used during labour, it tends to replace a hormone and therefore tends to inhibit the release of the natural substance. For example, the hormone oxytocin is commonly replaced by a drip of a synthetic substitute, while a painkiller or an epidural are substitutes for endorphins. A woman who has epidural analgesia and can watch the television during labour does not release the same hormones as the woman who gives birth by herself. If immersion in warm water is really a way to facilitate the

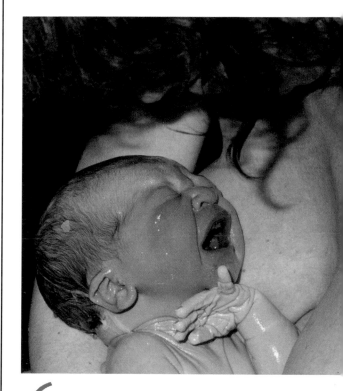

'Another advantage of giving birth in water is that the woman is always naked — she has nothing restricting her movements and can enjoy feeling the water against her skin. (If you have ever swum naked in the sea or in a pool, you will be aware of what a sensual pleasure it is.)'

' When the baby is finally pushed out of its safe, warm environment, it finds itself in one similar to that it has just left. It is then gently lifted into the warm embrace of its mother. The two naked bodies immediately make contact, the warm water gently lapping up over the baby's bottom and mother's breast. The atmosphere is quiet and peaceful; the mother seems instantly to forget the pain she has so recently suffered and just stares into her baby's eyes. Little hands explore the immediate surroundings, grasping at the air before falling on the mother's breast. The baby's head turns inwards towards that of its mother, finds a nipple and starts to suck. '

birth process, it is certainly not by introducing substitutes for natural hormones. We need urgently to explore the potential of non-pharmacological approaches.

It is easy to miss the meaning of the critical period surrounding birth when it is studied separately without reference to other episodes of sexual life. Today we can have a global vision of sexuality. All episodes of sexual life involve the same hormones and the same patterns tend to be reproduced. Oxytocin, in particular, can be seen as a female and male hormone which is involved each time there is a question of love, and not only as an agent inducing maternal behaviour just after a delivery. It has also long been known that oxytocin is necessary to contract the breast when the baby is sucking. Certain aspects of oxytocin release during lactation have been clarified recently. It has been shown that as soon as a mother perceives that her baby is hungry, her level of oxytocin increases. Furthermore, there is oxytocin in human milk. In other words, the breastfed baby absorbs a certain quantity of love hormone.

The role of oxytocin during sexual arousal and orgasm has also recently been brought to light. For example, when pigeons are

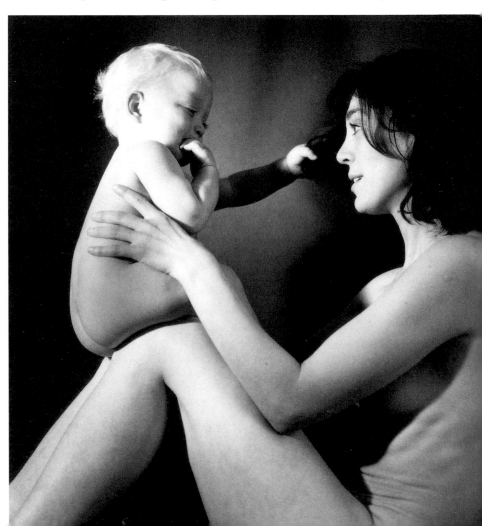

injected with oxytocin, the majority of them start waltzing, grabbing combs, mounting and mating. Now we have studies of oxytocin levels during orgasm among humans. Mary Carmichael from Stanford University evaluated oxytocin levels during masturbation and found that levels before orgasm were higher among women than men. Indeed, they were higher during the second phase of the menstrual cycle than during the first. During orgasm itself women reached higher levels than men. During male orgasm the release of oxytocin helps to induce contractions of the prostate gland, while in female orgasm it helps to induce uterine contractions which can help transport the sperm towards the egg. Modern physiology thus leads to a new vision of female orgasm. While it has been totally ignored by most known societies, female orgasm is now given a role in reproduction.

If we add to all these facts that sharing a meal with companions also increases our level of oxytocin, we must conclude that oxytocin is a hormone of love. It is probable that human beings can train themselves to release their love hormone very early during their fetal life. For example, it has been noticed during ultrasound scans that male babies can have an erection while sucking their thumb. It is also probable that babies can help initiate labour by releasing their own hormones.

While all episodes of sexual life are characterized by a release of an altruistic hormone, they also include a release of endorphins, which are both hormones of pleasure and natural painkillers. All mammals release endorphins when giving birth. The data now at our disposal have radically changed the basis of debates which were commonplace 40 years ago: is the pain during labour physiological or is it the result of cultural conditioning?

The role of endorphins during the birth process cannot be understood without reference to other episodes of sexual life. Each time we (mammals) do something which is necessary for the survival of the species, we are rewarded with a release of endorphins, which are also the hormones of pleasure. In modern physiology, pain and pleasure are two topics which cannot be dissociated. During intercourse both partners are rewarded with high levels of endorphins, and it is well known by some migraine sufferers that intercourse is a natural remedy for headache.

It is not, therefore, surprising that the reward system is also involved in lactation, which is necessary for the survival of mammals. When a woman is breastfeeding, her levels of endorphins peak at 20 minutes. The baby is also rewarded as there are endorphins in human milk. This is why some breastfed babies act as if on a 'high' after feeding. As the same hormones are

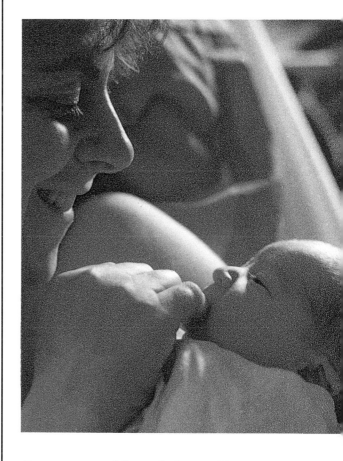

Eye-to-eye contact following birth is quickly established between mother and baby.

> After birth, water goes on to play a vital role in the bonding and caring process, which is closely allied with our feelings of love. The ritual of bathing an infant is usually an intimate time when the parent pampers the child and gives it undivided attention.

released during labour, lactation and lovemaking, it is not surprising that nipple stimulation, clitoral stimulation and lovemaking have been used to initiate or facilitate the birth process.

Not only are the same hormones involved in different episodes of sexual life, but the same patterns and scenario are also constantly reproduced. For example, during intercourse both partners release endorphins and oxytocin. The attachment between sexual partners seems to reproduce the pattern of the mother-baby attachment. This allows us to draw a parallel between male orgasm and the birth process. In the case of male orgasm, a passive phase of erection is followed by a 'sperm ejection reflex', which is under the control of nerves which use adrenalin as a mediator. In both cases — birth process and male orgasm — there is a short final phase which is active, violent and even aggressive. In many species the male tends to be aggressive at the time of the 'sperm ejection reflex', perhaps biting the female. Even the scientific terminology underlines the similarity between giving birth, breastfeeding and making love: 'fetus ejection reflex', 'milk ejection reflex', 'sperm ejection reflex'.

Among humans the facilitating effect of water can be seen as another link between different episodes of sexual life. It is not only during labour and delivery that water can influence the release of inhibitions — the erotic power of water is universally known and used. Restaurant owners, for example, create a relaxing atmosphere by placing an aquarium, a fountain, or sea paintings in the dining room. Traditional honeymoon destinations, such as Venice or Niagara Falls, also exploit the peaceful properties of water. All art forms, from painting and poetry to photography and music, have used the erotic power of water. In fact, it would take volumes to study how the cinema and advertising use the erotic power of water, often in a subliminal way.

Many breastfeeding mothers and members of such groups as the La Leche League are aware of the power of water and have noticed that in some circumstances the sound of it can be helpful. It can, for example, make sucking easier and at the same time be a way to reinforce the 'milk ejection reflex'. In addition, during the breastfeeding stage of infancy water seems to be a powerful medium to establish or strengthen affectionate links between baby and adult. This has been noticed by swimming instructors who specialize in teaching babies and is one of the reasons why the mother should be considered as the primary swimming instructor.

To look at sexuality as a whole has immense implications. It helps us understand that routine overcontrol of the birth process, as carried out in most cultures, probably influences other aspects

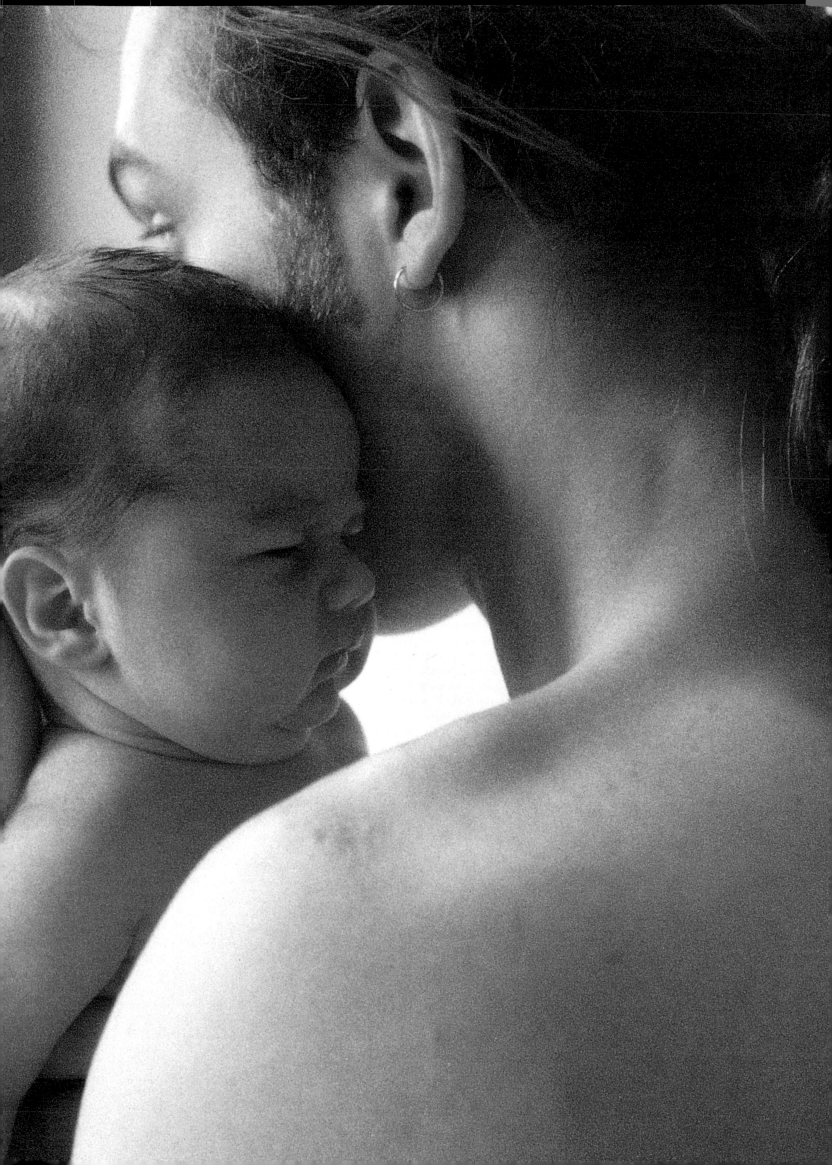

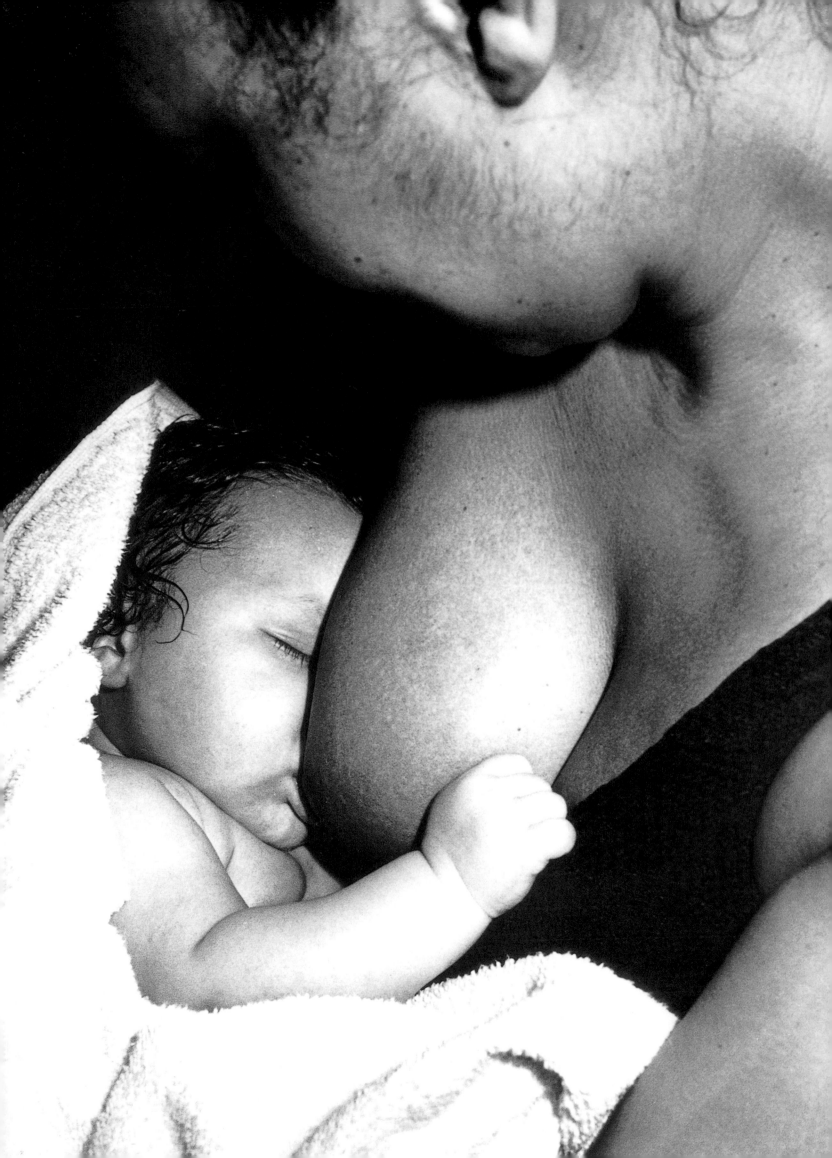

of sexual life. In addition, in societies where genital sexuality is highly repressed, women are less likely to have easy births.

Many new questions are inspired by a scientific vision of the capacity to love and its development. If the period surrounding birth is crucial, the attitude of most cultures, who have found excuses to interfere in the first contact between mother and baby and have denied the need for privacy, is more intriguing than ever.

It seems as if most cultures have challenged the maternal protective-aggressive instinct during the critical period following birth. By transmitting rituals and beliefs, such cultures have always managed to put the newborn baby in the arms of a person other than the mother. The most extreme cross-cultural interference has been based on the belief that colostrum is useless, even dangerous, while according to modern science, this thick substance the baby can take from the breast as early as during the hour following birth is highly precious. The end result of such beliefs and rituals is that the newborn baby is separated from the mother and may be given such nourishment as herb teas, water and sugar, elixir, cereals, honey, bone marrow, cow's milk or butter. There are exceptions, however, to these widespread practices, and all can be found in groups who share an unusual strategy for survival: they have to live in perfect harmony with the ecosystem. This is the case, for example, of the Eife Pygmies in the tropical forest of Zaire, or the Jackwash tribe in the Peruvian part of the Amazonian forest. They must develop the supreme form of love, which is the love of nature, the respect for Mother Earth.

Finally, focusing on the period surrounding birth and the power of water on human beings reveals the links between different aspects of love: love of oneself, the opposite of which is suicidal behaviour; parental love; love between sexual partners; love of 'thy neighbour'; love of humanity; and, at the top of the hierarchy, love for Mother Earth and life in general.

Our vision of the different forms of attachment to life, in the current scientific context, throws a new light on the non-verbal message given two millennia ago by the one whose mission was to promote love. He was born among mammals outside the human community, which suggests that there are circumstances when we have to accept our mammalian condition. It also suggests that there are situations in which human societies should not interfere too much. But to accomplish his mission Jesus needed more than that — he had to be born again in the water of the River Jordan.

If these non-verbal messages were the primal messages of Christ, we missed them and Christianity has never been tried. Is it too late?

'Birth seems to be one of the few instinctive bonds we still have with nature. If we can give children the best possible start in life, not necessarily material trappings, perhaps one day as a race we can truly learn the meaning of love and respect for the life force on which we all depend. '

Endorphins are the hormones of pleasure. When a woman breastfeeds, large amounts of endorphins are produced. The baby is also rewarded, as these hormones are present in human milk, which probably explains why many babies act as if on a 'high' immediately after feeding.

9 | Water from Birth to Death

OPPOSITE: *While the benefits of water are particularly apparent in infants, they are also important for the well-being of people at all ages. In fact, swimming is the only activity humans can pursue from birth to death.*

At the very end of his life I had the opportunity of meeting the actor Laurence Olivier. Even though he was old, sick and weak, he could maintain a certain degree of fitness by swimming every day in the pool of his country house. In fact, whatever wear and tear has done to their joints, many elderly people are discovering that they can still move easily in water. Swimming is the only physical activity humans can pursue from birth to death, and arguably the only one that can delay the ageing process.

As humans, we pay a high price for walking erect. The first part of our body to deteriorate is the spine. Signs of degeneration in the spinal column can be detected in people as young as 18. The discs, which act as shock absorbers, are made of an outer membrane containing a nucleus of thick jelly and are the first to deteriorate. Each time we undertake physical activity involving our weight-bearing joints — for example, running or jumping — pressure is applied to the discs, which tend to shrink, and the jelly is squeezed out. This gradually makes the discs flatten and our height starts to decrease in early adulthood. Further degeneration can make the discs rupture, bulge and press on the sensitive ligaments of the spine, or even the nerve endings. No wonder that low back pain is so common. Degeneration of the spine can be dramatically delayed if swimming is your main physical activity. When swimming the discs are not under pressure, so they can absorb the body fluids and push the vertebrae apart. Backache is the single most common reason for consulting a doctor or therapist and the cost of backaches can be expressed in millions of working days lost. In the case of acute lumbago, the best treatment I know is to take hot baths — as many as possible, as hot as possible and as deep as possible so that the body is totally supported by water. After a lumbago attack, and in the case of chronic low back pain, the contradictory aim is to maintain strong dorsal and abdominal muscles while simultaneously reducing the effects of gravity. For those with a tendency towards obesity, this means reducing body weight. It also means that swimming is the most appropriate sport. Backstroke is usually recommended to maintain a good balance between the main groups of the trunk muscles. While the maintenance of swimming pools is expensive, it is undoubtedly cost-effective in terms of public health. It will be even more cost-effective when people understand from an early age how important it is to spare one's spine and how this can be done.

There have been many changes in the approach to exercise during the 20th century. First, the health benefits were recognized, some focusing on the heart, blood vessels and lungs, others on the nervous system, on bone density, or on blood composition, while

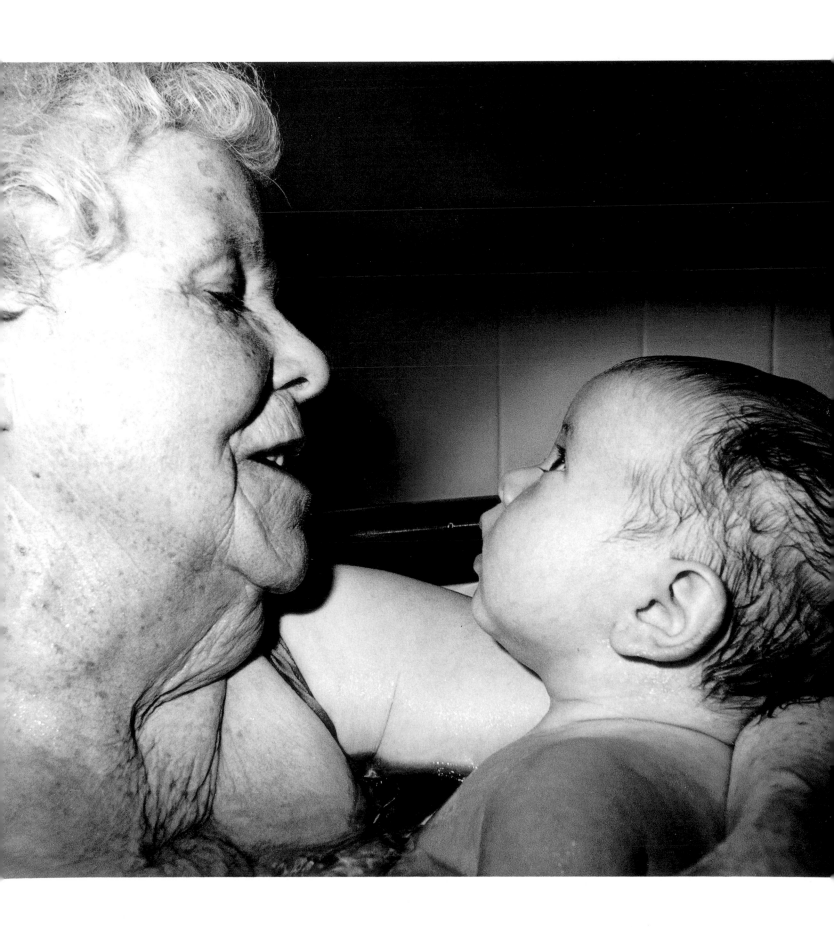

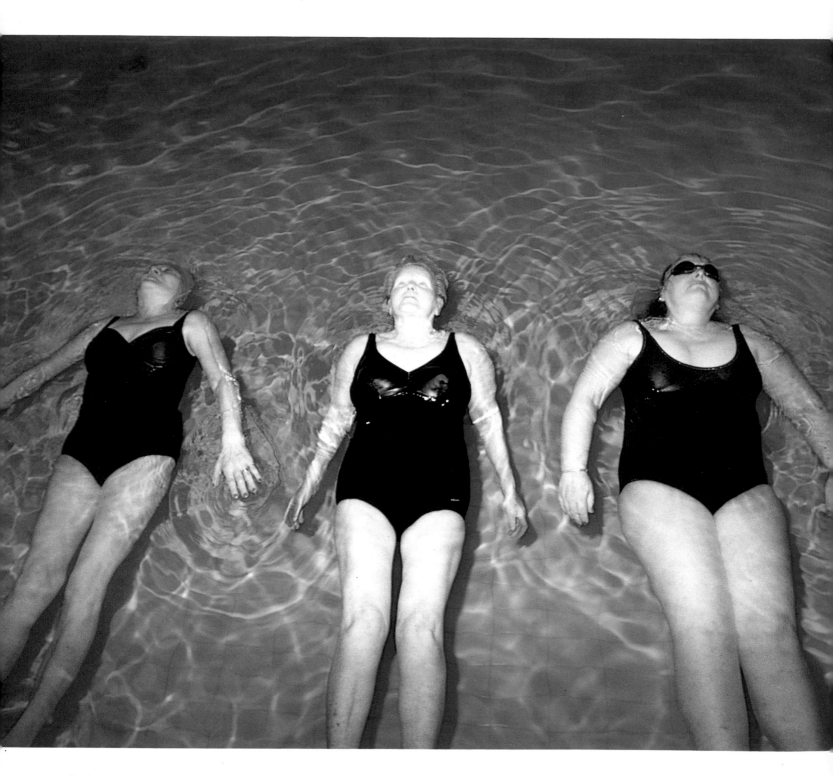

Hydrotherapy pools, which keep the water at a constant warm temperature, are ideal places for the elderly to swim.

others focused on muscular development and aesthetic considerations. Later it became commonplace to stress the need for aerobic exercises – short and intense activities that tend to increase the heart rate and breathing.

Today we are in a position to evaluate some of the negative effects of strenuous physical activity. We realize how vulnerable the human weight-bearing joints, such as the hips and knees, really are: they wear out more quickly if we use them often and intensively (a basic rule of mechanical engineering). As joints age, their shiny, smooth cartilage gets worn away, exposing the underlying bone, which becomes hardened. As deterioration progresses, movement becomes limited because the capsule of the joint is scarred and the surface of the bones uneven. Minor injuries may cause fluid to collect and the surrounding muscles start to waste so that the joint is less stable and prone to injury. Pain in a worn-out joint can be due to minor fractures of the bone surface, damage to the capsule or damage to the ligaments, but mostly it is due to muscle spasm.

In the 1960s, when I was a general surgeon, I used to perform the 'Voss operation', the aim of which was to eliminate all sorts of pressure in a damaged hip. First we had to cut the tendons of the muscles which were in a persistent and painful state of contraction. Then the patient was confined to bed for several weeks and the lower limbs kept in a system of continuous traction to eliminate any kind of pressure in the damaged hip. This operation sank into oblivion with the advent of hip replacement surgery. In retrospect its main interest has been to underline the paramount role of pressure in the wear on weight-bearing joints.

A large Finnish study of 2,448 male athletes has shown conclusively the link between overworking joints and the incidence of osteo-arthritis. The athletes were compared with a control group of Finnish men who, at the age of 20, were classified as fit for military service. All these men were monitored between 1970 and 1990, taking particular note of those admitted to hospital with osteoarthritis of the hip, knee or ankle. This study clearly demonstrated that international athletes involved in sports such as boxing, athletics and weight-lifting, are at higher risk of premature diseases of the weight-bearing joints. It is interesting that the study makes no mention of swimming. Obviously the researchers had assumed a priori that swimming is a very special physical activity. Unlike other sports, it can be either a relaxing activity or a real aerobic exercise.

Another advantage of swimming is that participants are not exposed to such risks as stress fractures, which are common in many other sports. In tennis, for example, it is easy to sustain a

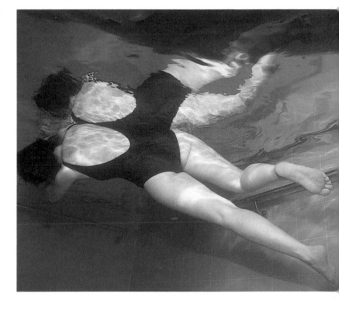

As humans, we pay a high price for walking erect. The first part of our body to deteriorate is the spine.

hairline fracture in a foot bone or lower vertebra without becoming aware of it till much later.

While it is well known that exercise can induce asthma attacks, particularly in children and young adults, it is now widely accepted that exercise is more beneficial than harmful to asthma sufferers. It is common sense that those who have experienced exercise-induced asthma should be steered away from sports such as football. Ideally, they should be encouraged to take up sports they can practise safely, such as swimming, water polo and diving. Exercise-induced asthma is almost unknown among swimmers. The main reason for this is that the air inhaled while swimming is usually warm and humid. As a general rule it should be remembered that those who have ailments unique to our species — varicose veins, haemorrhoids, inguinal hernia and obesity — can swim without fear of aggravating their condition.

OPPOSITE: *Whatever damage injury and age may have done to the joints, many elderly people are discovering that they can still move easily in water.*

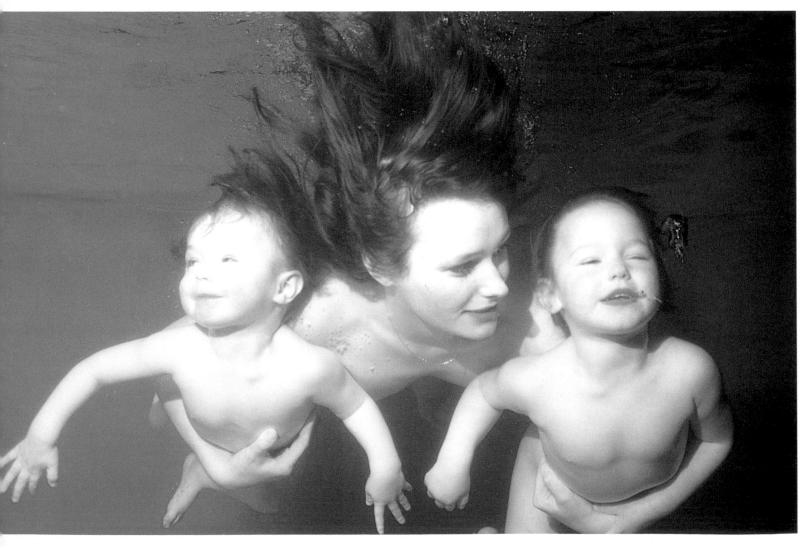

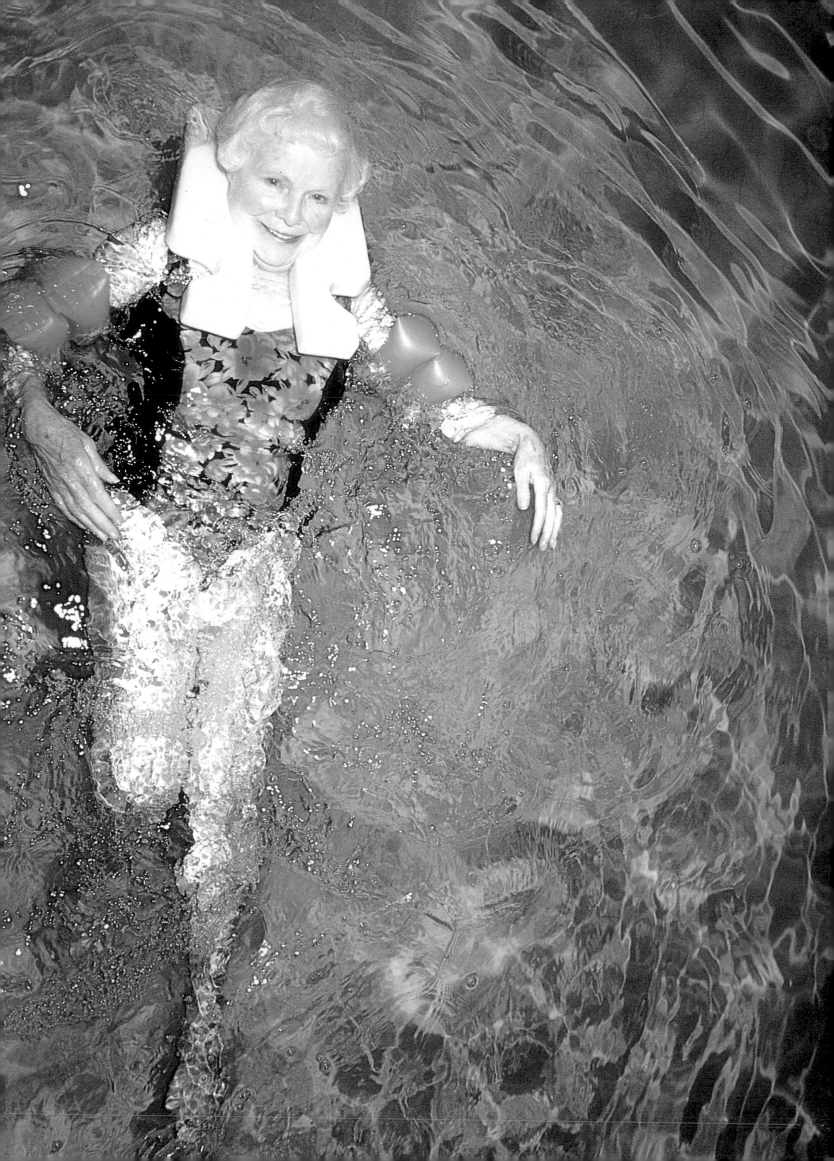

10 | The Healing Power of Water

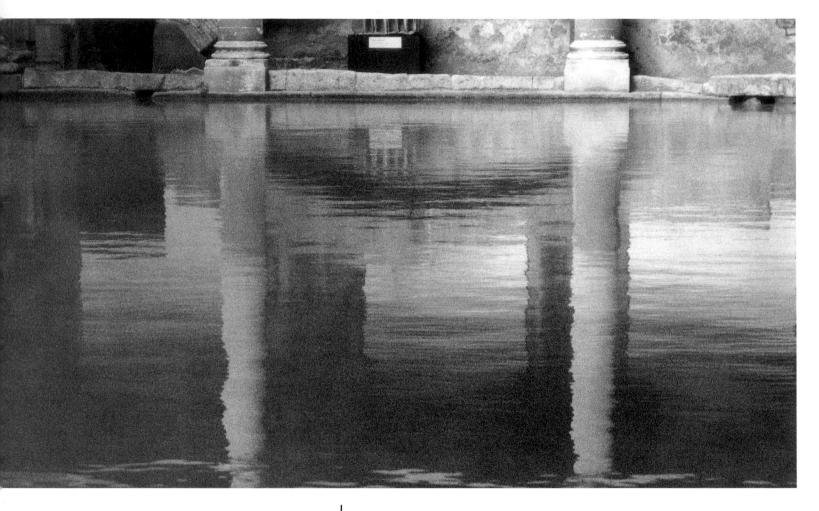

ABOVE: *The Romans were firm believers in the benefits of spring water, and were responsible for founding many spa towns in Europe, including Bath in southwest England.*

OPPOSITE: *A sacred spring, where many offerings were placed, ranging from pewter vessels to gold coins.*

Swimming can delay the ageing of our spine, our joints, our bones, our heart, our veins, ourselves. But water itself has healing powers.

When we are ill, we are like a baby: we need mothering. If our mother is not available, we can turn to a mother-substitute, such as a nurse. It is not by chance that the term 'nursing' derives from the Latin for 'nourishing'. Since we are all water babies, we can also turn towards water, the symbol of the mother. Is it surprising that water has always been associated with healing?

One has to ask why such a widespread phenomenon as the spa has not excited more sustained interest. Legend has it that in Japan a white heron led the first visitor, a wandering god, to the famous Tokarangawa hot springs. In fact, hot and cold springs play an important part in the traditional medicine of many cultures. Both the Chinese and the American Indians were familiar with their healing properties, while in ancient Greece the temples dedicated to Aesculapius, the god of medicine, were usually built

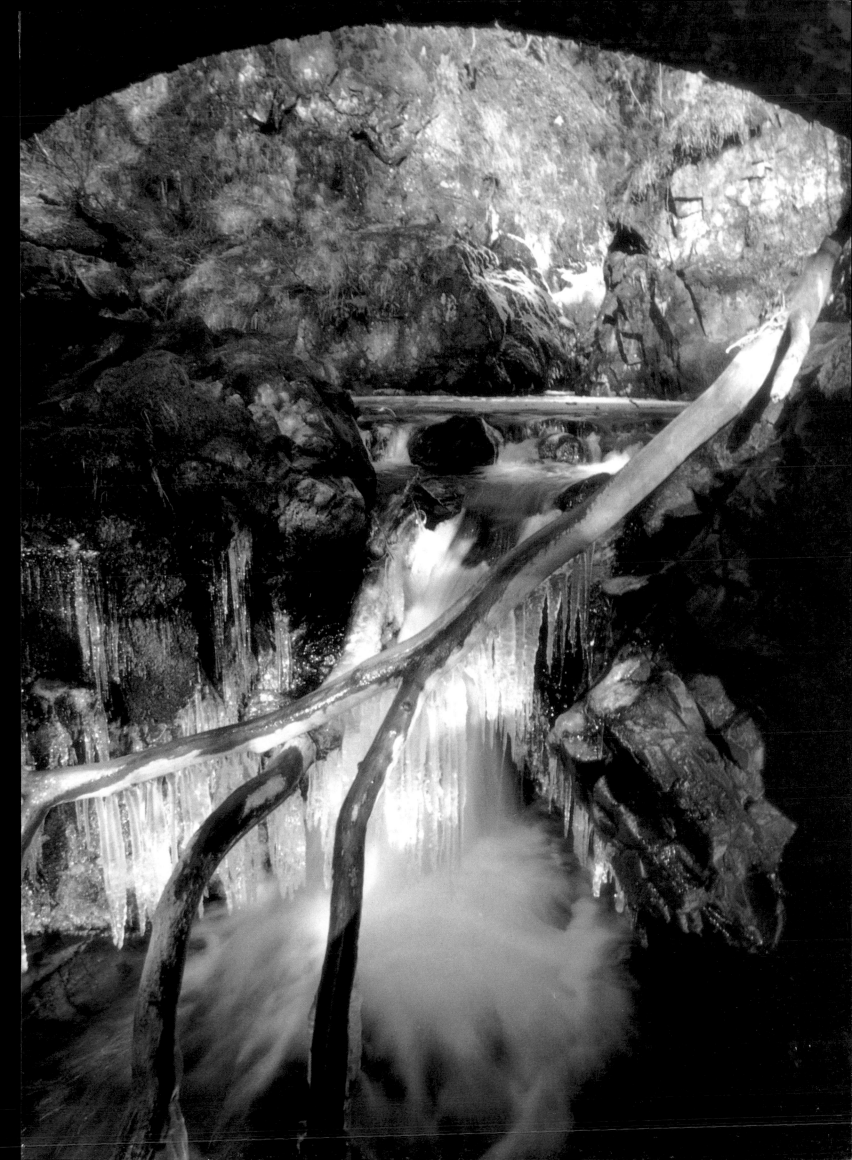

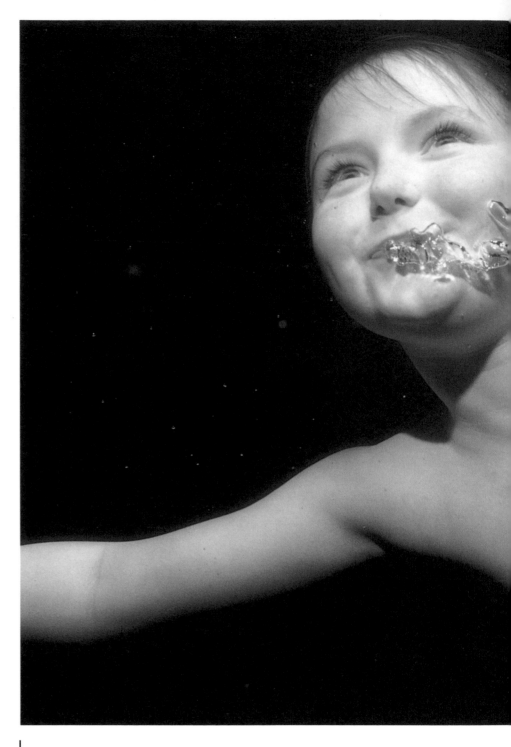

near springs known for their healing powers. The Romans were also firm believers in the efficacy of spring water, and were responsible for founding many spa towns in Europe. Bath, the famous spa in southwest England, was once known as Aquae Sulis, meaning the waters of the goddess Sul.

When I was studying medicine in Paris in the 1950s, I was convinced that the curriculum for my generation of medical students would be the last to include thermal spas. We had to learn about all those French towns whose names end in 'les thermes', or included the words 'eaux' or 'aigues'. With the enormous advances in pharmacology and surgery it was then commonplace to predict the decline and eventual disappearance of spas. In fact, quite the opposite has happened. Spas have developed to an unprecedented extent throughout the world.

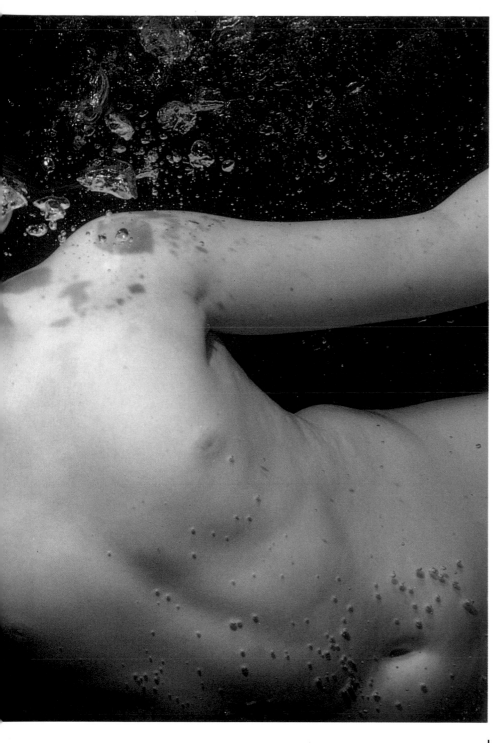

Children introduced to water at an early age enjoy its benefits throughout life. Young swimmers develop good, strong lungs and a healthy respiratory system.

In France spas have not only retained their allure and their reputation, but have also seen the emergence of thalassotherapy centres, where sea water is used for therapeutic purposes. In Germany there are more than 150 spas, and about six million people visit them each year. Hungary, which is rich in thermal springs, has been compared to the cover of a boiler, and that may be why this part of central Europe has been inhabited since prehistoric times. Thermal baths have survived the different phases of an eventful history: they were popular at the time of the Romans; then in the Middle Ages the first thermal hospital was built in Buda; after that the Turks renovated the oldest baths and now, in the age of modern medicine, the spas in Budapest are considered world leaders. In most continental countries the cost of a cure at a spa is covered by the national health service.

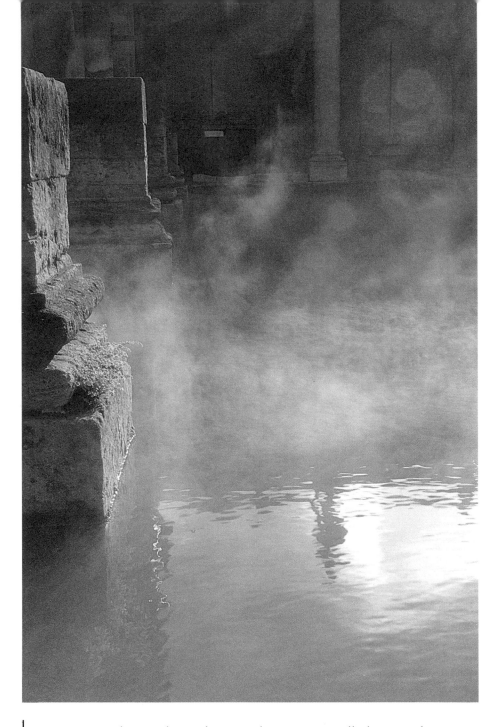

RIGHT: *Baths were places to socialize, as well as to enjoy the health-giving waters.*

OPPOSITE: *Sarah feeling the power of water and revelling in the freedom it gives her.*

In modern industrial Japan there is a so-called 'onsen boom'. Onsens are hot springs, and there are about 2,000 of them. In the United States there are more than 300 hotels, motels and boarding houses at Hot Spring National Park alone, which together can accommodate more than a million visitors every year.

The efforts of modern medicine to establish a rationale for the effectiveness of spas usually concern themselves with things like the composition of the mineral salt or gas, the temperature of the water, its radioactivity, or some other physical properties, such as the density and quantity of mud. Doctors, meanwhile, usually attribute the benefits of spas to the temporary change of environment and to being away from daily worries. They rarely talk about the water itself, or about the powerful impact of symbols on our emotional state and hence on our health.

Other water therapies have flourished alongside spas. Baths and wet packs, for example, have been used by some psychiatrists and psychotherapists, while some therapies use immersion to induce and exploit deep states of regression. Water has been used to help autistic children to socialize and its therapeutic power was

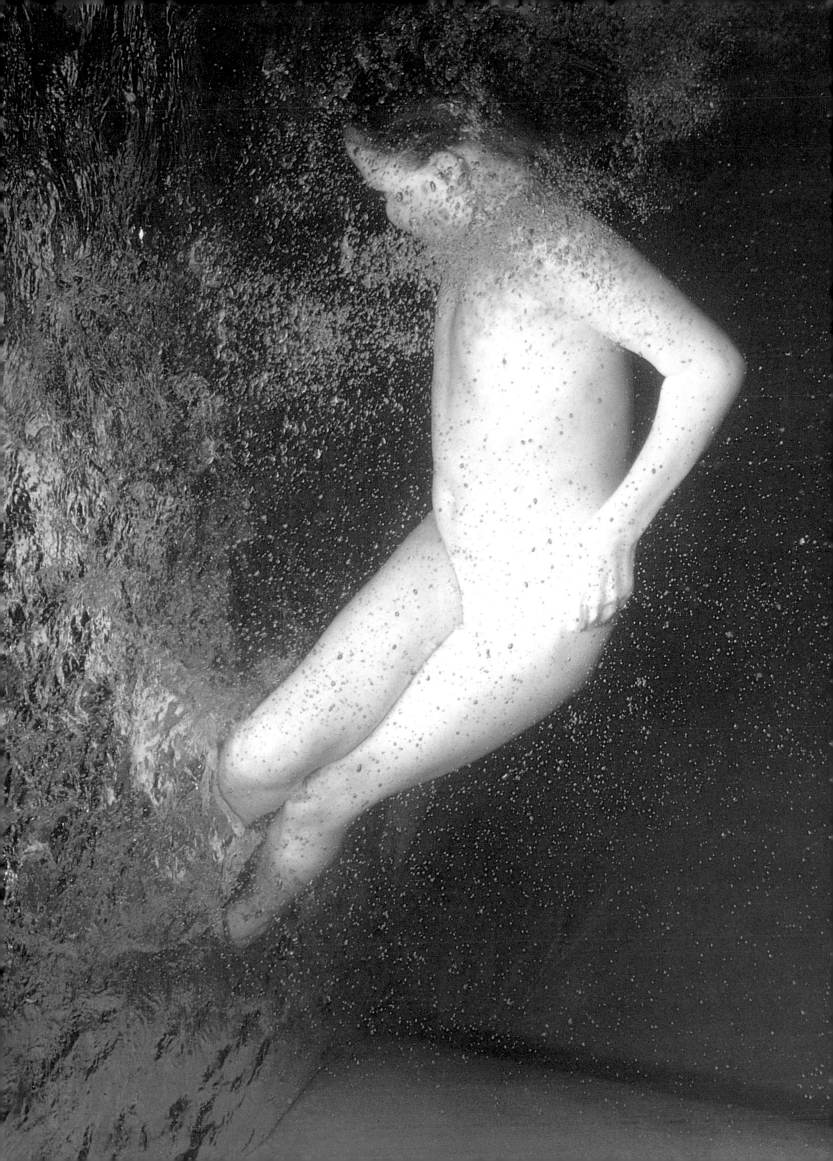

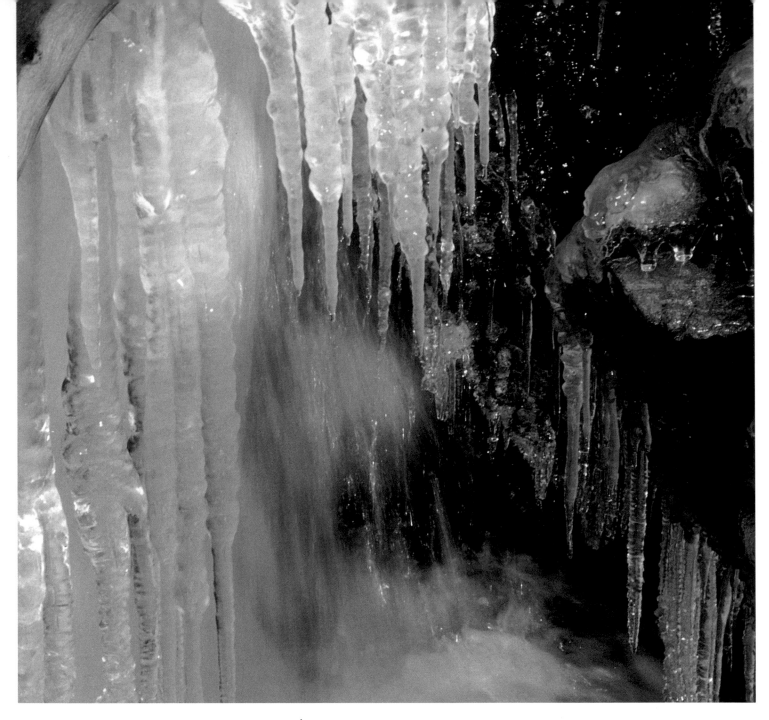

Water is a powerful natural element that can both give life and take it away.

also exploited by Candido Jacuzzi, who invented the whirlpool bath to treat his son's rheumatoid arthritis.

The power of water can work in subtle ways. Colour therapists say that a blue or turquoise environment induces a sense of calm, and some therapists also employ the healing power of sand. It goes without saying that sand and water are closely linked.

Only among sex therapists and researchers into human sexuality does it seem that the power of water is ignored. Leading figures in the field make no mention of the erotic power of water, despite the fact that it has been used through the ages.

Still in the field of sexuality, water has been given a practical role as a method of facilitating the physiological processes of labour. Only rarely has it been given the status of a healing agent needed by many civilized women who seem to have lost part of their capacity to give birth. The depth of the need probably depends upon cultural conditioning. In industrialized countries it is influenced by the childbirth practices of previous generations. For example, in 1933 in New York City the rate of operative deliveries (mostly forceps at that time) was 20 per cent. At the same time in

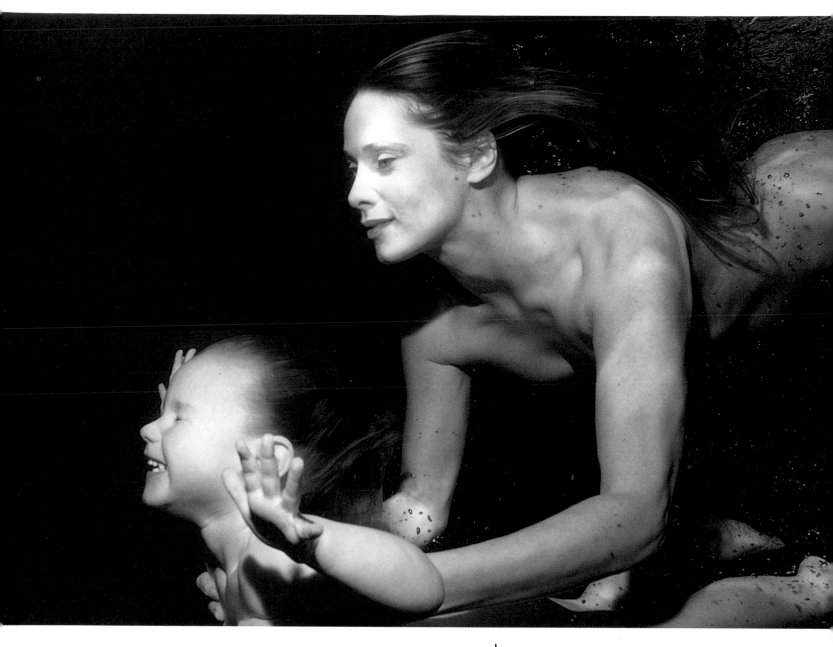

Sweden it was 3.2 per cent and in the Netherlands 1 per cent. Pregnant women living in 1933 New York would have been used to hearing about medically assisted births, while women in Amsterdam would probably never have heard of such a thing.

Perhaps deep-rooted memory, commonly called 'imprinting', plays a part. As the capacity to give birth unaided diminishes from generation to generation in developed countries, there is a tendency to exaggerate the role of medicine. Can the magic and even mystical power of water break the vicious circle?

It is, in fact, spurious to separate the healing power of water from its miraculous power, which has been used by all religions. In most societies religion and medicine are closely allied. The shaman has always been both a religious leader and a healer. It is worth remembering that only after his baptism in the waters of the River Jordan did Christ became a healer.

The fusion of religion and medicine in most societies makes sense at a time when scientists are in a position to study faith as a healing agent. The placebo effect is basically no different from the power of faith.

Swimming can delay the general ageing process, but water itself has healing powers.

11 | The Dolphin Connection

❝ My encounter with dolphins took place in Eilat, Israel, at Dolphin Reef. Lauren and I met the organizers previously when they had attended the 'Dive Show' in Birmingham in 1993. They were interested in the project we were undertaking and agreed to let us go out there and take some pictures.

Dolphin Reef is a large area of open sea approximately 10,000 square metres (12,000 square yards) and reaching a maximum depth of 16m (50 ft). The area is sectioned off from the rest of the sea by a series of nets. It plays host to seven bottlenosed dolphins – five originally taken from the Black Sea (via the Soviet Academy of Sciences), one from Japan and one baby which was born within the complex. ❞

BELOW AND OPPOSITE: *According to Greek mythology, dolphins were originally humans who lived in cities along with mortals before exchanging the land for the sea and adopting the form of fishes.*

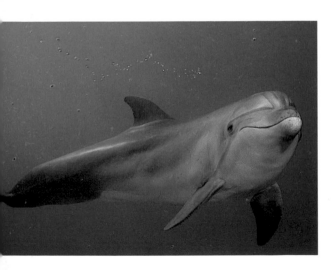

Not only does water have mysteries and mystical power, so do its inhabitants. The human-dolphin connection is as old as our historical memory and is cross-cultural. How did it come about?

Traditional fishing cooperation might be at the roots of this connection. Until recently in Mauritania there was actual complicity between fishermen and dolphins, with both sides helping to round up the catch. It seemed as if they had struck a deal to share the fish. In view of this close relationship, it is not surprising that in that culture killing a dolphin was tantamount to killing a man. Similar fishing complicity has been reported in ancient times in the Mediterranean by such people as the Greek author Oppian and the historian Pliny. Coastal-dwelling Aborigines in different parts of Australia have also fished in harmony with dolphins since time immemorial. This may help to explain the 'Monkey Mia' phenomenon. Monkey Mia, on the west coast of Australia, is the only place in the world where children can easily meet families of friendly dolphins in shallow water.

The human-dolphin connection seems to be based on mutual trust. Using their powerful snout like a ram, dolphins could easily kill a man, but they don't do it. On the other hand, they wouldn't hesitate to kill a shark threatening a baby dolphin.

Dolphins never attack humans, but there have been countless stories of them saving lives. In 1993, for example, two men and a boy set out in a small boat from Le Conquet in order to gather shells on a nearby islet. Too late they noticed that the weather was changing. Heading northeast, they tried to get home but the sea was so rough that the small craft was in imminent danger of capsizing. Then a school of dolphins appeared and clung to the craft as if trying to make it stable. After a while, and to the sailors' bewilderment, the dolphins started pushing the boat south, towards Camaret. Eventually all became clear when they realized that the dolphins had led them into calmer waters, probably saving their lives.

Such a story might be regarded as pure fabrication had there not been tales of dolphins saving men from drowning and steering ships to safety reported by people all over the world and through the ages. Documented examples appear in such diverse places – classical Greek texts and Polynesian tales, for example – that no one could claim collaboration or a conspiracy to mislead. Whatever aspect of the human-dolphin connection we consider, the cross-cultural similarities are striking. In places as far apart as possible on this planet there are legends of humans changing into dolphins and vice versa. According to Greek mythology, dolphins were originally humans who lived in cities along with mortals

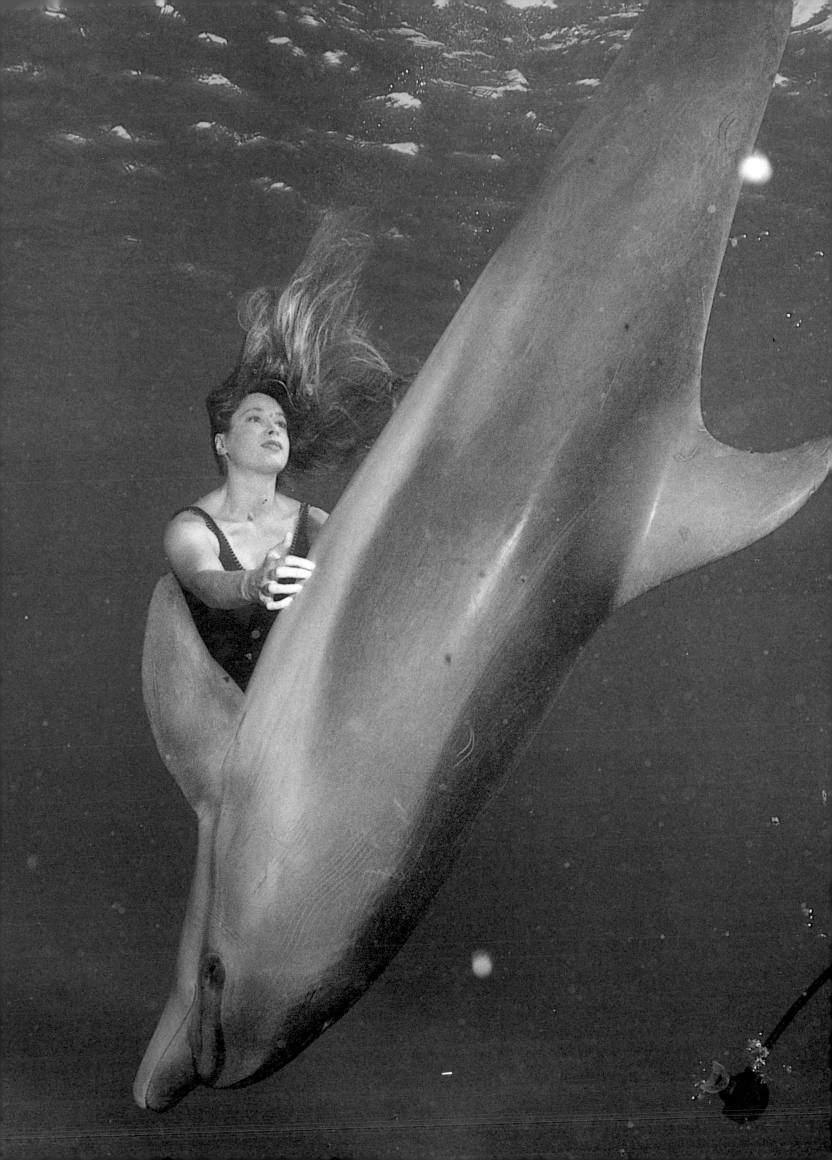

before exchanging the land for the sea and adopting the form of fishes. The beliefs of the Maoris in New Zealand are basically the same, and their tradition has it that a dolphin is a 'human being of the sea'. Similarly, the natives of an island in the Gulf of Carpentaria, northern Australia, believe that humans and dolphins have a common ancestor: she is the mother Ganadja, who one day took the shape of a human being. The natives of another island in the same gulf call themselves the 'Dolphin People' and believe that their shaman is a dolphin who has chosen to reincarnate as a human being. In fact, the shaman-dolphin connection is another striking cross-cultural phenomenon. More generally speaking, dolphins have always been seen as divine creatures or divine guides for humans. Given the separateness of their origins, all these beliefs

'Lauren and I were to work with a team of three divers: Mosheko who acted as Lauren's buddy breather, Yair, who was to be my buddy, and Naomi, who worked with the dolphins and helped attract them to us.

It was important to familiarize ourselves with the dolphins before shooting started, so we went for an introductory dive. We swam around for a while simply enjoying the marine life, but could see no dolphins. After a while, I heard a clicking noise and suddenly we seemed to be surrounded by dolphins. They swooped in between us, then disappeared, only to appear again at lightning speed. Being so close to these creatures made me fully aware of their huge size and immense power.

It was clear that the dolphins were in a playful mood, and as we relaxed into the spirit of the game, my arms reached out to touch and stroke them. My feelings can only be described as sheer joy as my fingers felt the texture of their porcelain-smooth skin.

And then they were gone! The game was over and an expanse of what suddenly seemed like empty water stretched out in front of us. We returned to shore with big grins on our faces. '

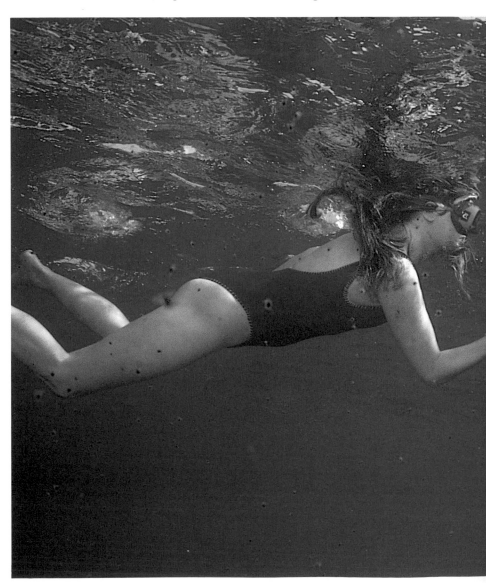

become highly significant when they are brought together.

The ancient and apparently universal interest in dolphins means that the current fascination for them cannot be seen as transitory or merely fashionable. Of course, the recent resurgence of interest does owe something to publicity about modern fishing practices which endanger the species and provoke outrage around the world. But it also suggests that humanity is suffering from a guilty conscience at transgressing deep-rooted moral rules.

The most spectacular modern form of fascination for dolphins is the desire to swim with them. As Amanda Cochrane and Karena Callen pointed out in their book *Dolphins and Their Power to Heal*: 'the extraordinary experience of swimming with wild dolphins fired a fascination which turned into a near obsession for

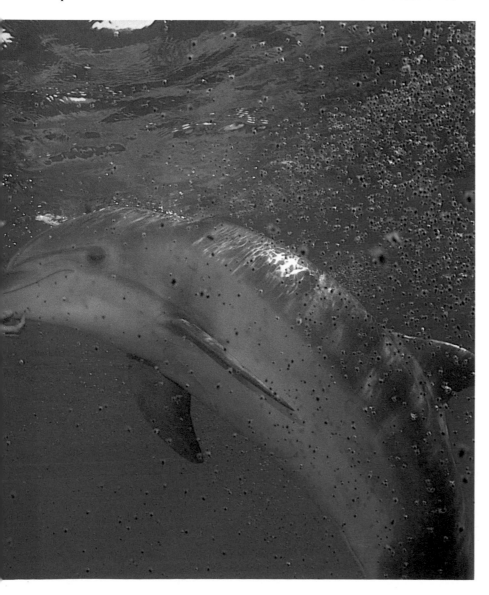

The human-dolphin connection seems to be based on mutual trust. Dolphins have never killed man.

' Swimming and playing with dolphins is one thing — photographing them is another. First I had to distance myself as I wanted Lauren to get their attention. Then there were all the technical and physical hurdles to overcome.

One of the main problems we encountered was the dolphins' frequent lack of interest — it was as if they knew we were there to work rather than play. Although their natural curiosity brought them over to us, there were certain days when we surfaced having achieved nothing. It wasn't until Naomi, who has a particular rapport with the dolphins, came along with us that we were more successful.

Much of the success of Dolphin Reef lies in its philosophy that contact made with humans, other than during training sessions, is based on the free will of the dolphins to approach. There is no reinforcement by feeding during these approaches.

The dolphins do, in fact, have a private area where swimmers and divers may not enter, and frequently they do retreat to this particular section of the reef.

Training sessions with the dolphins take place four times a day. The trainers position themselves on floating rafts, which are accessible only by boat, and visitors can watch from a pier. The sessions last about 30 minutes and the dolphins are fed between performing a few jumping exercises. The trainers do, however, play down the connection of food reinforcing the human contact. '

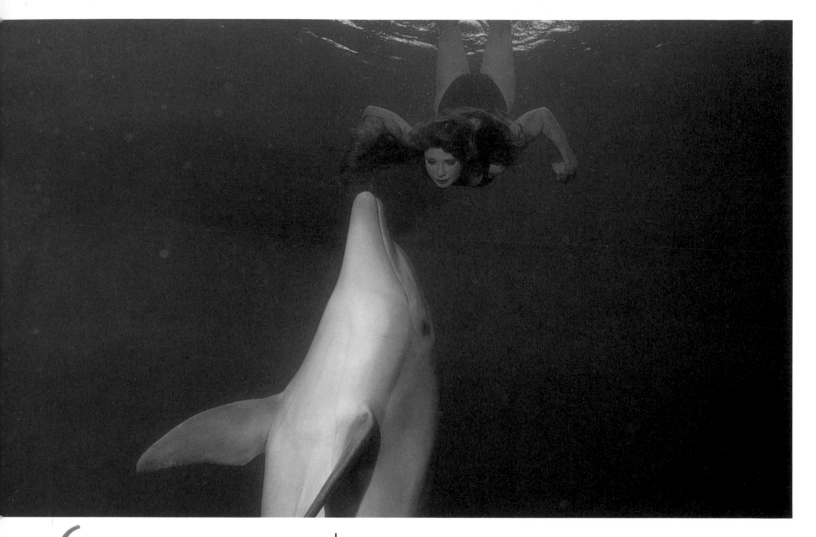

'   As Lauren and I became familiar with the dolphins and people that worked within the reef, I couldn't help but notice what a positive feeling radiated from the site. The energy seemed to get inside us, lifting our spirits, even when the going was tough.

This positive energy that the dolphins exude has been the subject of careful research over several years. Dolphin Reef itself has become a centre for working with people who have a wide range of disabilities, including Downs Syndrome, cerebral palsy, depression and autism. People who enter the reef have no reward other than the freedom the water provides and contact with the dolphins, but the benefits are real. I experienced the joy myself, and also saw the obvious rapport between Lauren, who had recently suffered a personal loss, and one particular dolphin. It was wonderful to imagine the effect dolphins have on people who are trying to overcome huge difficulties in life. '

us both'. Others whose relationship with dolphins have inspired widespread interest include the French diver Jacques Mayol, subject of the film *The Big Blue*, and internationally known 'dolphin people' such as Estelle Myers and John Hunt. The desire to swim and dive among dolphins has been enhanced by factors as diverse as the writings of experts such as John Lilly and Horace Dobbs, by television programmes, by disapproval of dolphinariums and, not least, by opportunistic travel agents.

Meeting dolphins in their natural environment is a new form of tourism which is developing dramatically in places such as Kaikoura in New Zealand. Increasing numbers of humans and dolphins are involved in these encounters, organized by companies which need a permit from the government. The strategy of these companies is based on the works of dolphin expert Wade Doak. The main step is to establish a trusting relationship between a crew and a group of dolphins through regular meetings, during which tacit rules are established and interest is stimulated by creative games. In Kaikoura the dusky dolphins were the first involved. Now bottlenose dolphins and Hector's dolphins join the parties. Encounters with wild dolphins are also well organized in the Bahamas and in the Gulf of Aqaba in Israel.

Encounters with dolphins need not be restricted to the framework of tourism and holidays. They can also be encountered in a healing context. In 1972 Dr Henry Truby, from the World Dolphin Foundation in Key Biscayne, Florida, observed that

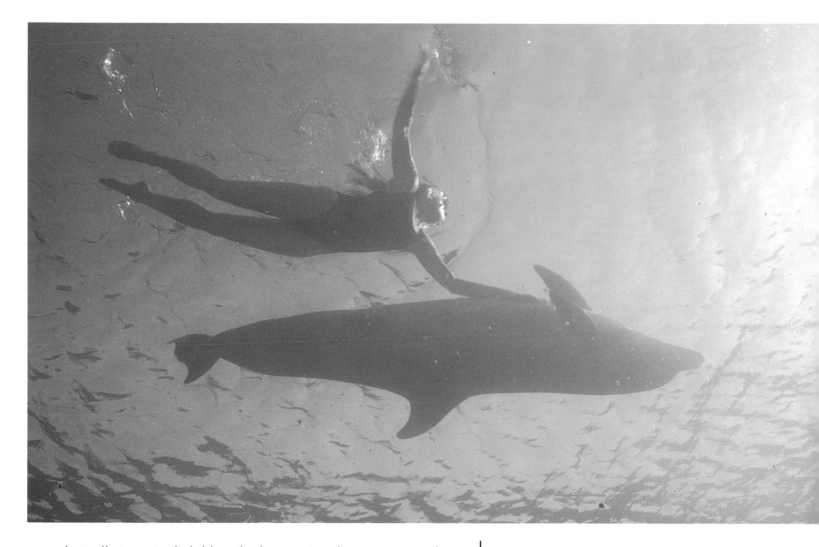

neurologically impaired children had exceptional responses to close contact with free-swimming dolphins. At the same time Betsy Smith, a specialist in autism at the University of Florida, noted unexpected positive responses from the interaction between a usually aggressive, unruly adolescent dolphin and a retarded adult called David. While the dolphin became gentle, patient and attentive, David, who was usually very cautious near the water and slow to adapt to new stimuli, immediately waded in and began talking with the dolphin, stroking him and playing with him.

Dr Truby, Betsy Smith and another expert in autism met and laid the foundation of a research project. The place was to be a deep artificial cove in a canal in Key Largo, from which the dolphins could return to the ocean when they wanted. Here, autistic teenagers could be in contact with the dolphins, either staying on a platform where the dolphins would be playful with them, or entering the water itself. The first observation was that the dolphins persevered in trying to communicate with autistic children, remaining friendly and joyful even when faced with unresponsiveness, which ordinary pets wouldn't do. At several conferences on the human-animal bond Betsy Smith presented positive conclusions. One of the most significant was that the encounters and their after-effects were found to be life-enriching by the parents of all who participated.

It is also in the 1970s that dolphin enthusiast Horace Dobbs in Great Britain became intrigued by the sudden recovery — after

'Dolphin Reef is a remarkable place. Although it is a commercial venture and the dolphins are essentially captive, this particular group was, in fact, rescued from harsh conditions. They are clearly happy (dolphins do not usually breed in captivity) and are obviously loved and cared for.

Of course, it will be a great day when there are no captive dolphins. Until that day arrives, places like Dolphin Reef offer a kinder solution. With luck their work will encourage people to realize that next time they see a dolphin, it should be in the wild.'

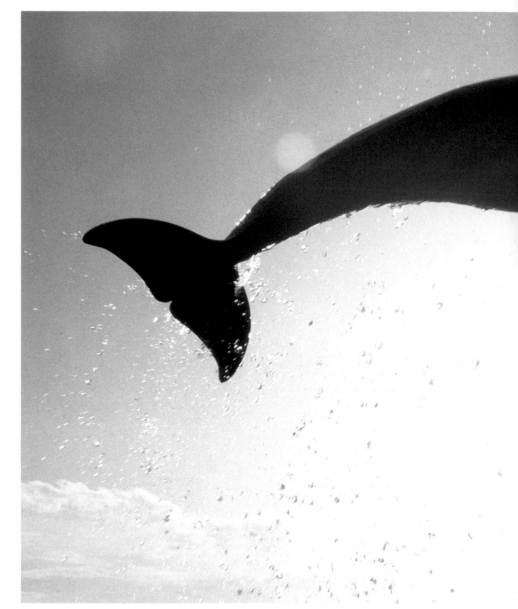

swimming with a dolphin — of a lifeboat mechanic who was close to a nervous breakdown. A few years later in Wales, while leading a group of people who wanted to meet a dolphin, Dobbs noticed that the dolphin spent most time with a man who was in a state of deep depression and had heart disease.

After several similar observations, Horace Dobbs set up a series of projects, including Operation Sunflower, the aim of which was 'to study friendly and ethical ways to take advantage of the healing power of dolphins, without exploiting them and disturbing their usual way of living'.

Another programme, designed by Dr David Nathanson in the USA, is based on using dolphins and music to capture the attention of mentally retarded children. Such a programme, however, implies that the dolphins would have to be trained. The future of dolphin therapy depends on how ethical questions are posed and answered.

Several theories have been put forward to interpret the healing power of dolphins. For example, it has been assumed that dolphins can sense imbalances in subtle bioenergy fields and can influence them. It has also been suggested that swimming with

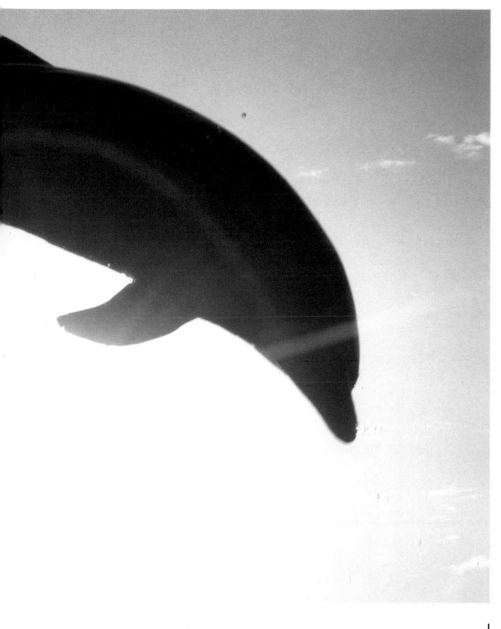

Dolphins are playful and inquisitive creatures. Being in close proximity with them over a period of time fills one with a sense of well-being, perhaps because they always seem to be smiling.

dolphins may trigger alpha brain waves, which are linked with serenity. Other theories stress the healing potential of sounds emitted by the dolphins. This is reflected in the work of swimming instructor Denis Brousse in Lyons, who uses sounds similar to those chanted by Tibetan monks when he is in the water with neurologically handicapped children.

In fact, whatever the method of interaction, the healing effect of dolphins is not wholly surprising; it might even be anticipated if what is already known is taken into account. For example, we know that to take the initiative is health enhancing, while a state of submission is the typical disease-creating situation. For this reason, a therapy chosen on the initiative of the patient has a higher probability of working.

This attitude probably also accounts for the success of alternative therapies at the very time when pharmacology and surgery are more effective than ever. Let us recall the experiments with rats receiving electric shocks: what made the rats ill is not the number or the intensity of the shocks but the fact that, when receiving such shocks, they could neither fight with a companion nor escape – they had to submit. We also know about the

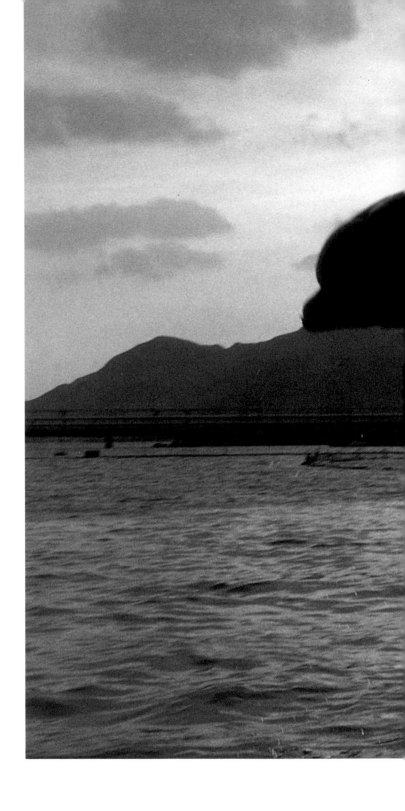

' I particularly enjoyed the last session of the day, when I regularly accompanied one of the trainers to a raft and photographed the dolphins playing and jumping. It was wonderful to get so close to these fascinating animals. '

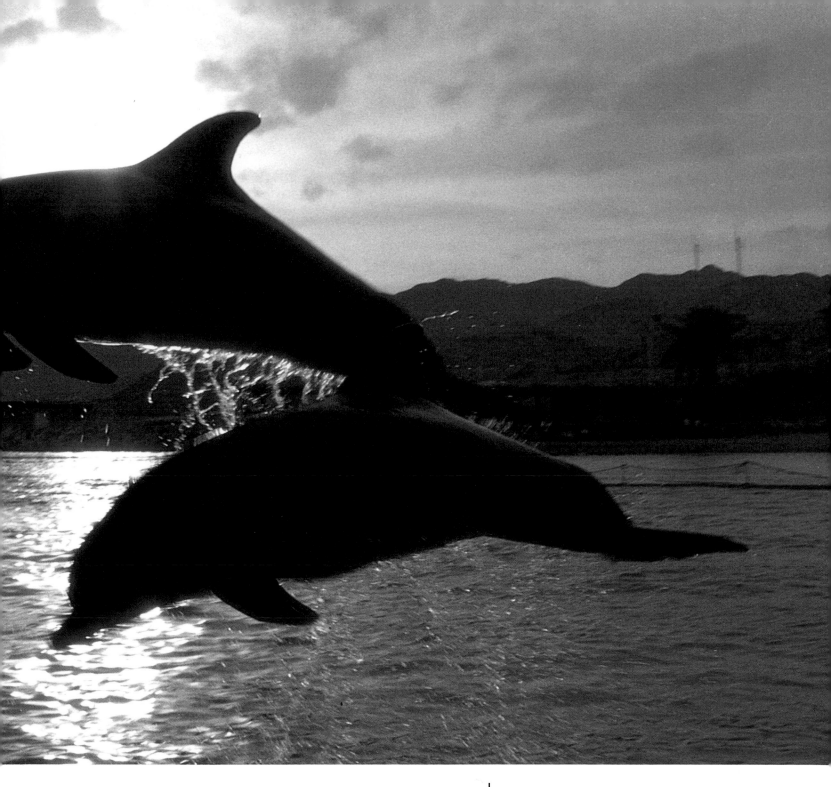

therapeutic power of water and the deep-rooted cross-cultural fascination for dolphins compared with other sea mammals. We know too that dolphins are joyful animals and that joy is contagious. Moreover, there have been countless studies demonstrating the positive influence of animals on our health, especially when the human being and the animal are known to each other. This is a point which has been stressed by several therapists: 'dolphin therapy' seems to be more successful when the dolphin and the human have established a relationship.

The friendly and inquisitive nature of dolphins makes us warm to them and give them human names, just like real friends. Some of the most famous dolphins are Jean-Louis in Brittany, Jojo in the Bahamas, Percy in Cornwall, Fungie in Ireland, Simo in Wales, Freddie near Newcastle, Jotsa in Montenegro and Dolphy in the South of France. Personalizing our relationships with dolphins is no different from humanizing them.

Early evening at Dolphin Reef is a wonderful time: the dolphins are usually in playful mood — literally jumping for joy.

12 | Are We Marine Chimps?

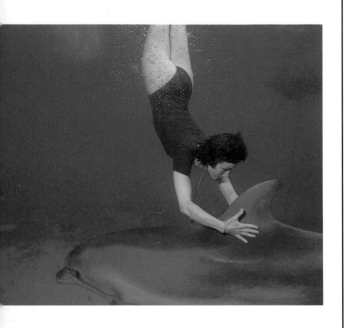

ABOVE: *While many land mammals have close cousins in the sea, all our close cousins are on the land.*

OPPOSITE: *A baby's early attempts to remain upright show its physical resemblance to our primate ancestors.*

Where do our closest relatives live? After focusing on the intriguing and deep-rooted human-dolphin connection, you might be surprised at the unambiguous answer given by modern scientists: while most land mammals have close cousins in the sea, all our close cousins are on the land.

This is the teaching of molecular biology, a discipline that has developed dramatically over the past 10 years. By comparing molecules that are present in all species, biologists are now able to measure the genetic distance between two species of mammals and establish how closely related they are. Furthermore, they can evaluate how much time has passed since two related species shared a common ancestor.

Whatever method they use, and whatever molecules they study (nuclear DNA, mitochondrial DNA, or amino-acid sequences of proteins), molecular biologists now claim that we are — so to speak — chimpanzees. We share 98.4 per cent of our genetic material with them. The distance between us and other chimps is less than the distance between gorillas and chimps. It is even less than the distance between two particular species of gibbon. According to recent evaluations, humans and other chimps separated 'recently' from their common ancestor, which is no more than 6 to 8 million years ago.

Next time you visit a zoo you will probably spend a while in front of the chimpanzees. You will look at them with renewed curiosity and notice dozens of obvious major differences between us and these apes in cages. (How is it that lay people can instantly recognize so many differences between two species while molecular biologists can distinguish so few?) The more the gap between us and chimpanzees is reduced, the more intriguing become the morphological and behavioural features that distinguish humans. The reasons for the differences stem from a very simple rule confirmed by countless observations: when two species are genetically close to each other, most morphological and behavioural differences are usually explained by an adaptation to different environments. Conversely, animals that are not genetically related can have many common points if they are adapted to the same environment. For example, New World (American) vultures and Old World vultures look so similar that they have been confused by zoologists. In fact, biologists now know that the American birds are genetically related to storks, while the Old World birds are related to hawks. Their close resemblance stemmed from leading similar lifestyles in similar environments.

We know to which environment non-human chimpanzees are adapted. The common chimpanzee is adapted to the tropical

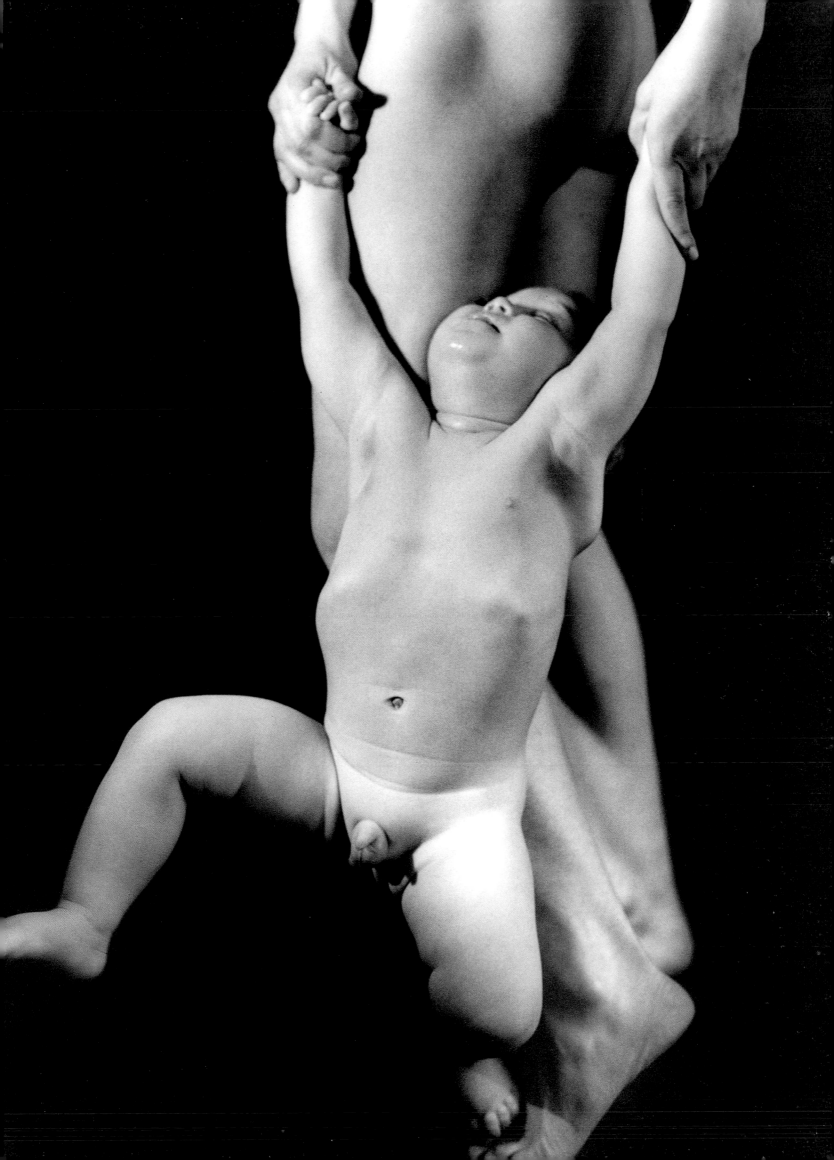

rainforests of Central Africa, while the pygmy chimpanzee is adapted to the flooded forests south of the River Congo. Paradoxically, the environment humans were originally adapted to is still a mystery. One way of fathoming this mystery is to take one by one all the features that make humans different from chimpanzees. This method would disclose an environment which is not incompatible with all these features. Such an approach would suggest that there has been a time in our evolution when we were adapted to the coast.

Let us start with the most intriguing difference between humans and chimpanzees, which is the size of the brain: ours is four times bigger than that of our cousin. Nutritionists have an interpretation to offer for this disparity. They have recently realized that there is a family of fatty acids which is essential for the brain. These are the so-called omega 3 polyunsaturated fatty acids. Although they have a precursor in green land vegetables, the polyunsaturated forms are found in human milk and in the seafood chain only. 'Fish is good for your brain' is no longer just an old wives' tale. A large brain — compared with that of genetic relatives — indicates adaptation to the sea. Sea mammals, especially cetaceans, have bigger brains than their cousins on land. This fact provides a new perspective on the primate *Homo*. The human brain combines the structure of the apes' brain with the development of the sea mammals' brain. The nutritional needs of humans in terms of fatty acids suggests that we are primates adapted to the coastal seafood chain. In fact, modern nutritionists claim that humans cannot be totally healthy without occasionally consuming seafood. While, in the past, mothers guided by mere experience knew that cod liver oil was good for their children, there are now scientific reasons for examining the beneficial effects of fish oils in conditions as diverse as heart disease, skin complaints, rheumatism, obesity, diabetes, multiple sclerosis, mental diseases and cancer.

It was this current understanding of our nutritional needs that prompted me to conduct a study of pregnant women who eat a lot of sea fish, especially oily varieties such as mackerel, herring, pilchard, sardines and salmon. We need to know at which point this diet improves the health of pregnant women — and therefore of their babies — influences the way they give birth, and influences the rate of premature births. As the fatty acids of the seafood chain are supposed to facilitate the development of the brain, this long-term project has to follow up the children.

While our large brain sets us apart from apes, another feature peculiar to humans is the expression of emotion with tears.

This is not incompatible with an adaptation to the sea, since marine iguanas, turtles, marine crocodiles, sea snakes, seals and sea otters weep salt tears, while land mammals have no tears or any sort of nasal salt gland. Their existence in humans might be interpreted as a vestige of an extra mechanism for eliminating salt.

The general shape of our body, with the hind limbs forming an extension of the trunk, is not incompatible with aquatic adaptation, since it makes us streamlined, like all sea mammals. The shape of our body is also well adapted for walking and running on two feet. This upright stance is not incompatible with life on the coast: it is easier to keep vertical when moving in shallow water. Human babies, for example, can stay erect and walk in water before being able to walk on dry land.

The absence of hair covering the human body has often been considered as the most striking difference between man and ape. The zoologist Desmond Morris started his famous book *The Naked Ape* by wondering why, among 193 living species of primates, only members of the human species were naked. A hairless body is not incompatible with adaptation to the sea. In fact, all completely aquatic mammals (dolphins, whales, dugongs), many tropical semi-aquatic mammals, stellar sea-lions and elephant seals have hairless bodies. Mole rats, which live in tunnels, are the only naked land mammals. While it may be argued that elephants and rhinos are hairless land mammals, they are very aquatic and need mud cover to protect their naked skin.

While the human body has no hair to keep it warm, it does have a layer of fat under the skin — another feature that is not incompatible with adaptation to water. All medium and large species of sea mammal have a layer of white fat that provides buoyancy, streamlining and insulation against cold, but on land the fat layer tends to reduce speed and can act as a heat trap. This leads on to considering how we regulate our body temperature. First, it must be stressed that our body temperature is normally 37ºC, which is lower than that of most land mammals (horses are 38ºC, cattle and guinea pigs 38.5ºC, rabbits, sheep, dogs and cats 39ºC, goats 39.5ºC). The comparatively low human body temperature is something we share with sea mammals. Similarly, our body temperature fluctuations are less than 1ºC, while they are 5ºC or more among many other land mammals.

To control our body temperature in a hot environment we sweat. In fact, of all mammals, we have the highest sweat production. Sweating has long been considered an enigma, or a mistake of nature, as it depletes the body of large amounts of water and salt. This makes no sense at all to those who consider human

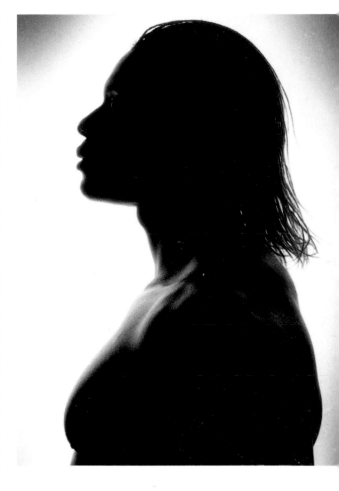

According to modern nutritionists, a large brain indicates an adaptation to the sea. Modern nutritionists claim that humans cannot be totally healthy without occasionally consuming seafood.

beings to be first and foremost primates who keep the characteristics of a fetus or a baby until adulthood. (In fact, the human baby does not control its temperature by sweating for the first few weeks following birth.) New interpretations of this sweating mechanism become possible when we consider human beings as primates adapted to environments where water and salt are freely available. In fact, fur seals are the only mammals — apart from humans — who sweat when they are overheated on land: they sweat on their naked hind flippers. Therefore, sweating is another human trait which is not incompatible with adaptation to the sea.

Nose and throat characteristics also offer points of contrast between man and chimp, and even between man and other land mammals. First, we have a prominent nose. Interestingly, the only primate which also has a prominent nose — the proboscis monkey — lives in the coastal wetlands of Borneo and is an excellent distance swimmer. It uses swimming to escape the cloud leopard, which hunts at night and is reluctant to follow its prey into the sea. A long nose is obviously an advantage when swimming or diving, as it deflects water from the nostrils. Another major characteristic of the human face is that we have large empty sinuses on each side of the nasal cavities. The air in these cavities undoubtedly makes our skull lighter, even buoyant, and this too is not incompatible with adaptation to swimming.

Still in the area of the upper respiratory tract, there is another intriguing difference between us and other chimps, and even other land mammals. Our larynx is low, which gives us the choice of breathing with our nose or our mouth. It also allows us to speak. The advantage of a low larynx when swimming is that we can fill our lungs in a second between two strokes. Sea-lions and dugongs are also characterized by a low larynx.

Once again, this is a human feature that is not incompatible with adaptation to the sea. Oddly, however, human beings are not born with a low larynx. Young babies are nose-breathers, which allows them to suck and breathe at the same time. It is around the age of 4 months that the larynx loses contact with the palate and begins to descend.

As mentioned in Chapter 1, 4 months is also the age when the neocortex is taking over from the primitive reflexes, which include automatic swimming movements. After a certain age, and a certain degree of development in the neocortex, human beings are distinguished by being able to exercise voluntary control over their breathing. Our new brain can decide, for example, to stop our breathing for a few seconds or, on the contrary, make us breathe deeply and quickly for a while. This is what makes articulated language possible. It is also what makes adult swimming behaviour special.

Let us compare how different primates swim. Monkeys swim instinctively and very well. Humans can also be very good swimmers once they have learned and if they are well trained. But most apes are afraid when in water and drown very easily, either sinking motionless, or panicking. They appear to be mid-way between the instinctive monkeys and the well-conditioned humans. Their neocortex is more developed than the monkeys' but less so than ours. Where swimming behaviours are concerned, they are like human babies during the critical phase. As swimming is a learned process among adult humans, it is highly dependent upon early conditioning. That is why there is a great diversity of aquatic behaviours among humans. Negative conditioning can induce a chronic fear of water, and even the incapacity to swim. Finally, thanks to their voluntary control of breathing, humans have the potential to be the best divers and the best swimmers among primates. Sponge and pearl divers, for example, usually descend to about 20m (60ft) and can stay under water for several minutes. Well-trained swimmers have the stamina to swim back and forth across the Channel, while the speed of an Olympic short-distance swimming champion can be compared with the speed of a fast walker. As we can see, voluntary breath control can be turned to advantage in terms of adaptation to the sea.

While there are many sexual behaviours among land mammals, some general rules do apply. One of these rules is that the male tends to approach the female from behind. In this , humans are special. In most known cultures humans copulate face to face. Moreover, they are orgasmic. Once again, these features are not incompatible with adaptation to the sea, as dolphins and whales also copulate face to face and are very orgasmic. The human vagina shares a number of characteristics with the vagina of sea mammals: both are long and oblique, and both have a hymen. In sea mammals the hymen is supposed to be a barrier preventing water from entering the vagina. In women it has been demonstrated that the human vagina is waterproof — an important consideration at a time when many women relax in a bath during labour.

In terms of sexual behaviour, pygmy chimpanzees are an exception among the apes because they copulate face to face and both male and female have orgasmic reactions. Interestingly, pygmy chimpanzees are adapted to the swamps of tropical forests and have been seen swimming. It seems that they have reached a higher neocortical development than the common chimpanzees.

To complete this study of the features that make humans special let us make a short detour to examine our blood. In

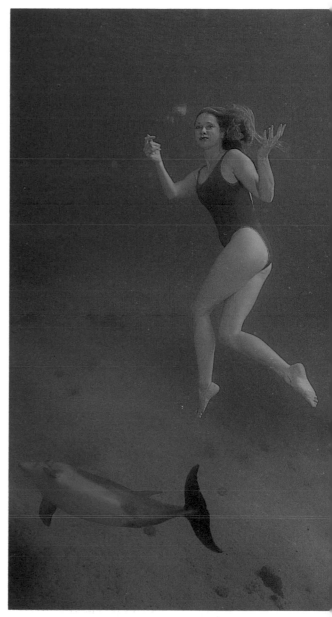

Lauren beckons the dolphins towards her: usually they are only too delighted to play.

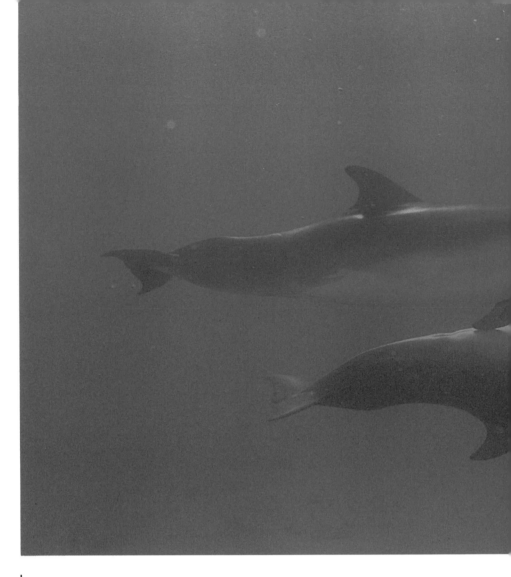

humans there are 5 million red blood cells per cubic millimetre, versus 7.3 million in a chimp's blood, while the percentage of haemoglobin (red pigment) per cell is 15 for humans and 12 for chimps. Like us, marine mammals have a reduced number of red cells and a high haemoglobin level, so here are yet more signs that humans are closer to sea mammals than the apes.

Another obvious area of comparison between humans and chimps is manual dexterity. Both have hands with five fingers and both can perform a wide variety of manual tasks. Humans, however, have the advantage of a highly developed area of the brain which specializes in movements of the hands and fingers. This allows us to achieve things like playing the piano or using a typewriter, which a chimp could never do. This leads on to comparing our hands with those of the chimpanzee. The main visible difference is a triangle of skin between thumb and forefinger, which prevents us from making an angle of more than 90 degrees. This triangle of skin, which looks similar to the webbing on a duck's feet, is another feature that is not incompatible with adaptation to water. The same kind of observation can be made regarding our feet: the big toe is jointed to the others in man, but is separated in chimps.

This leads me to mention one of the most common congenital abnormalities (or particularities) human beings can have, namely webbing between the second and third toes. This is highly significant because a congenital abnormality that takes the form of adding a feature usually means that the feature had a reason for being there during the evolutionary process.

One feature that suggests our adaptation to the sea is the fact that humans copulate face to face and are orgasmic. Dolphins and whales also copulate face to face and are highly orgasmic.

Perhaps in the future we might improve our understanding of human nature by trying to interpret the most common anatomical abnormalities in our species, compared with those of other species. A study by the Dutch anatomist Cornelis Van Die involved the dissection of 38 seals. Not only did he find many common points between the heart in humans and seals, but he also found that four seals had a narrowing of the aorta just beyond the point where the arteries diverge towards the head. This finding is interesting because such a narrowing of the aortic arch is one of the most common vascular abnormalities among humans. It results in more blood being sent to the head and upper limbs and less to the lower limbs. That is why cold feet are among the first symptoms of the abnormality. Among seals this condition can be seen as an adaptation to diving, as it is a means of ensuring a sufficient blood supply to the heart and brain.

Cornelis Van Die and the health philosopher Machteld Roede together were able to make the kind of connection scientists often miss because they are too specialized. They found a link between the narrowing of the aorta (coarctatio aortae) and a Norwegian myth according to which seals are sinful sailors. Punished by the gods, they are condemned to live at the mercy of the water, tide and wind. But the seal who saves the life of a sailor is rewarded, changing into a beautiful princess and becoming the sailor's bride. This woman has beautiful dark eyes and a beautiful body, but her feet are always cold...

There is still much to learn from congenital abnormalities and myths...

13 | When *Homo* Becomes *Sapiens*

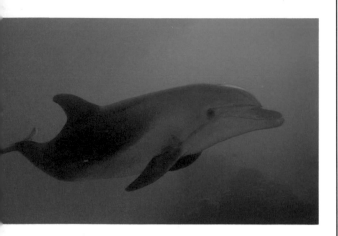

'Know thyself'. These words were written on the temple of Apollo in Delphi and ascribed to the Seven Wise Men. The knowledge of oneself is recognized as the basis of wisdom. If the vision of *Homo* as a marine ape asserts itself in the near future, this will be the biggest breakthrough in the quest of our origins — that is, in the knowledge of ourselves — since Darwin. It also means that two names will emerge from the ocean of scientific and technical advances that have occurred in rapid succession during the 20th century. These names are Alister Hardy and Elaine Morgan.

In 1960, in a modest article published in *New Scientist*, Sir Alister Hardy, a professor of marine biology at Oxford University, proposed what is now called 'the aquatic ape theory'. It is a revolutionary theory of the emergence of man, according to which our direct ancestor was a primate who went through a semi-aquatic phase. Hardy, however, did not promote his hypothesis, preferring to wait for fossil evidence to confirm his views. While waiting, he devoted the end of his career to research into other features of man's nature.

Meanwhile, the writer Elaine Morgan mulled over the questions raised by Hardy and eventually introduced the general public to his theory via her books *The Aquatic Ape*, *The Descent of Woman* and *The Scars of Evolution*. Each book is an opportunity to update the theory and to adapt it to a constantly renewed scientific context.

Elaine Morgan also organizes conferences, bringing together scientists from a great variety of disciplines, and it was through such an event that I first met her. She invited me to participate in a conference of the British Association for the Advancement of Sciences in Southampton in 1992, and at a study day in San Francisco in 1994. With geologist Leo La Lumiere, Elaine Morgan has proposed a possible scenario for the emergence of man. According to this scenario, a group of apes might have been trapped on an island at a time when part of East Africa was probably covered by the sea. In the circumstances they had to adapt to the new environment and it has been well known since Darwin that life on islands tends to accelerate the process of evolution. (It was in the Galapagos Islands of the Pacific that Darwin collected most of the information that supported his theory about the origin of species.)

There are now numerous approaches which converge to support the aquatic ape theory. It is this convergence of data coming from numerous horizons that makes us take the hypothesis very seriously. When reviewing the main features that make man different from the chimpanzees (see Chapter 12), I was

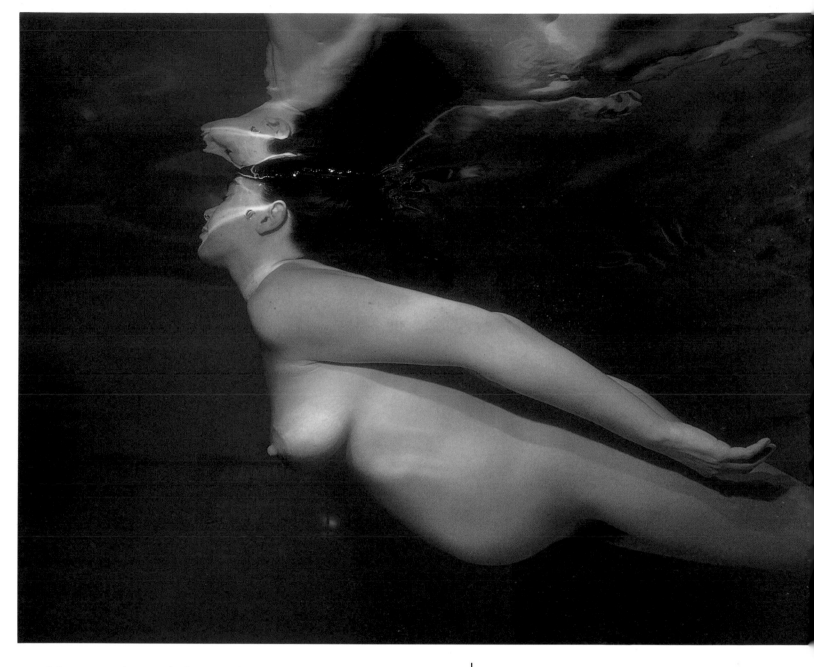

careful to state that each feature showed 'no incompatibility' with an adaptation to the sea. I wanted to stress that no single feature is sufficient to support a new theory, but all of them brought together become highly significant. The difficulty when a radically new synthesis is proposed is that each expert, viewing it from his or her own specialized field, does not see the separate strands and therefore cannot understand the reason for this new theory. An outsider, such as Elaine Morgan, is in a better position to have a global and more balanced perspective.

The last decade of the 20th century is also a time when an increasing number of scientists have dared to free themselves from the imperialism of fossil hunters and to look at the emergence of man with new eyes. Until recently, fossil hunters were considered to be experts in human origins, and the only ones with authority to propose theories. Today there are good reasons to consider fossil hunting as a parallel rather than superior method of understanding the emergence of man. There are many reasons why fossil evidence alone is inadequate:

In 1960 Sir Alister Hardy proposed the 'aquatic ape theory', suggesting that our direct ancestor (a primate) went through a phase when it was adapted to both land and sea.

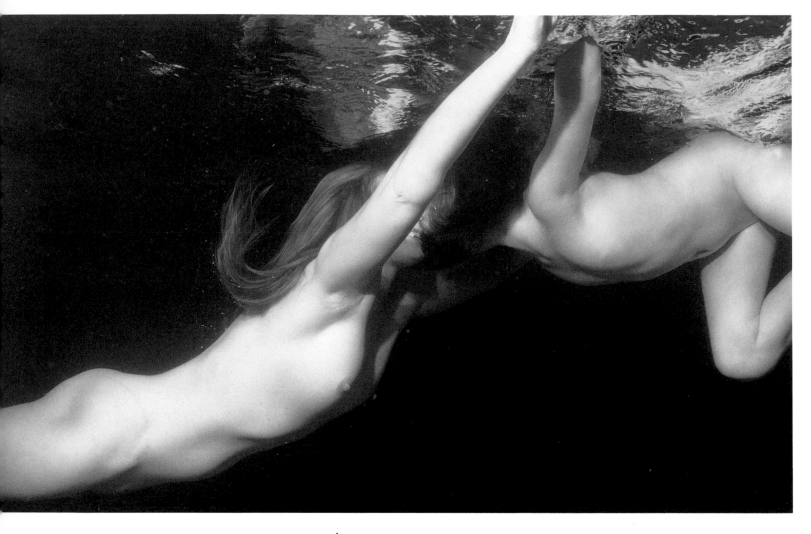

In order to enhance our knowledge of ourselves it is vital to be aware of which environment we were originally adapted to.

● When human fossils are found, it means first that the geological conditions are absolutely exceptional. The French geologist Jacques Varet, who has a good knowledge of East Africa, enumerated all the geological conditions that have to occur together so that a hominid fossil has even a tiny chance of being detected one day by a palaeontologist. East Africa is so exceptional from a geological point of view that it is not surprising that fossils of hominids living 2 or 3 million years ago were found there. But we have to be cautious before suggesting that the emergence of humanity occurred in this part of the world.

● Only hard parts of the body, such as the teeth, skull, jaw and long limb bones, can be preserved and found in fossils. In addition, fossils are often distorted by earth movements during their long burial. As many adaptive characteristics concern the soft tissues only, it is impossible to distinguish the fossils of a tiger from the fossils of a lion.

● According to molecular biology, humans and chimpanzees separated around 6 to 8 million years ago. But there is a virtual fossil void between 10 and 3.5 million years ago!

Elaine Morgan has understood the importance of multiple approaches in the study of human origins. She has the ability to detect significant data from disciplines as diverse as geology, palaeontology, palaeoanthropology, primatology, comparative anatomy, comparative physiology, comparative pathology, methodology and, not least, molecular biology. Today it is clear that

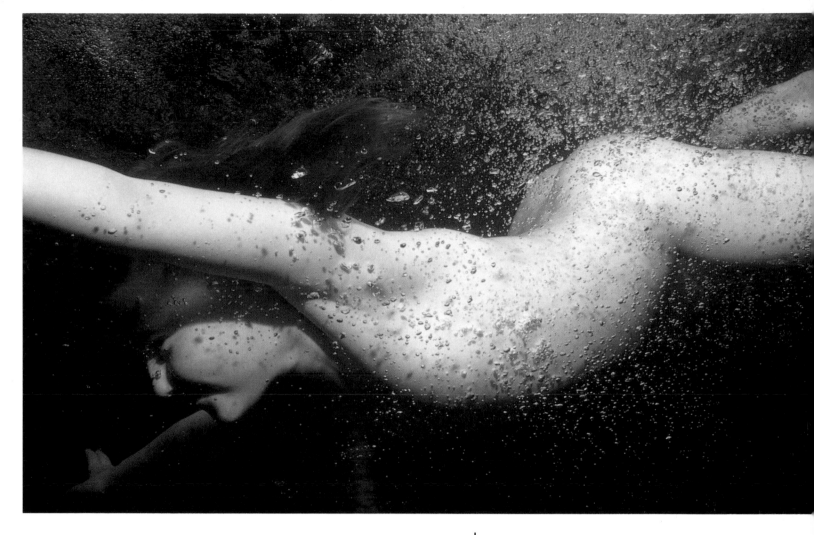

the golden gateway to our past is through the study of body molecules, particularly those of our genes. This will certainly lead to all the dominant theories being reconsidered. The following example has drawn the attention of Elaine Morgan.

All African primates carry the so-called 'baboon-markers', a type of genetic scarring that suggests the primates had to adapt to a virus which was both pervasive and threatening. This marker is not carried by Asian primates or *Homo*, so there are good reasons to reconsider whether man even originated in Africa. Molecular biology makes us go back to square one. I am inclined to stress a radically different — but not contradictory — approach to exploring our past. It is the interpretation — or the reinterpretation — of myths, legends and sacred texts. We should seriously decipher our collective unconscious as the mental inheritance of all mankind.

We are at a stage in our history when we must combine all possible perspectives to improve our knowledge of ourselves. There is a vital need to rediscover to which environment we were originally adapted, but this is a thorny task. While animals adapt to an environment to survive, humans transform the environment and adapt it to their needs.

We now realize with dread how far we have gone in that direction, becoming like travellers who have lost contact with their point of departure. The time has come to draw up an inventory of our original needs. Today, 'know thyself' applies to humanity as a whole. Let us dream of a time when *Homo* becomes *sapiens*.

Unlike other animals, humans tend to transform and adapt the environment to their own needs. We have become like travellers who have lost contact with our point of departure.

Appendix
How the photographs were taken

Nikon has a long history of underwater camera production. Jacques Cousteau designed the first. It was called the Calypso, and was a big success in its day. Today, there are three options in Nikon camera equipment:

• A land-based camera which can be used in an underwater housing
• The Nikonos V, specially developed for underwater use and very popular with divers interested in photography
• The Nikonos RSAF — the most advanced underwater system to date from Nikon.

The Nikonos RSAF was the main camera used for the photographs in this book. Given the difficulty of framing and composing many of the shots, its autofocus and large LCD (liquid crystal display) screen were to prove invaluable.

The camera usually comes as a complete kit with body, three lenses (20-35mm zoom, 28mm and 50mm), extension brackets, SB 104 flash unit and battery recharger. Complete reliability and absolute watertightness at depths of up to 100m (300ft) — the limit Nikon guarantees — probably accounted for the overall weight of the case. The camera body alone weighed nearly 2kg (4¼lb)

Despite this, I found the RSAF extremely sophisticated, with every aspect of its design and operation having been thoroughly thought through. Loading was simple. Once the cartridge had been inserted, the motor drive automatically wound it on, and provided the film was DX-coded, the ISO was also set automatically. The loading chamber was set inside the back, the outer being the watertight seal which, when opened, revealed a lightweight inner door to the loading chamber. In this area too were the battery chamber, the rewind switch and the rear curtain flash sync switch.

It should be mentioned here that the Nikonos RSAF is the first underwater SLR (single lens reflex) camera, so its setting controls are very similar to most land-based cameras of that type, but with a few added extras. Apart from the shutter release, there is an aperture control button to the far right of the top plate (rather than on the lenses themselves) with settings from F2/8 to F22, plus intermediate settings. Below the shutter release is a power focus lever, and set to the left of the HP finder is a versatile focusing system with options. All information for taking a picture is electronically passed through the camera body to the lens. The three lenses

Jessica holding the Nikonos RSAF — the world's most advanced underwater camera.

are supplied with bayonet fittings and are dedicated to the RS. Only the 50mm lens is also suitable for land pictures, the optics on the other two being solely for underwater work.

With the flash system attached, the whole apparatus felt heavy and awkward on land, but underwater it became a sturdy and well-balanced instrument that I could manoeuvre quickly and with relative ease. The larger-than-normal viewfinder provided exceptional clarity, not normally associated with underwater photography. This proved to be a particular bonus for me, as my subject matter was so diverse, and I had to be so quick when composing my pictures. The brightly illuminated readouts on the LCD screen provided me with all the information I needed, and this was another detail of the camera I particularly appreciated.

The flash unit that accompanies the RSAF is the SB104, a powerful flash with a variety of modes and functions. Choosing the right mode for a particular need can be tricky at times, but for the water baby shots, in particular, I tended to use the matrix-filled balanced flash in conjunction with the aperture-priority mode of the camera. Correct shooting ranges gave the babies a natural appearance without making them look artificially lit.

When I started photographing the babies, I used the 50mm lens. I soon realized, however, that I had to retreat too far away from the subject to fill the frame successfully and that the subsequent skin tones were pale and washed out. It was the 28mm lens that was to prove the most efficient for my needs.

The main thing that one learns when doing the sort of underwater photograph in this book is that careful planning is essential. The babies could stay under water for up to 10 seconds maximum, so it was important that the mothers and instructors knew what I was trying to achieve before I went under the surface.

If photographing water babies was a challenge, photographing people swimming with dolphins was to prove even more so. For these shoots I went to Dolphin Reef in Israel, a privilege accorded to few photographers. The team I worked with included Lauren, whose underwater abilities proved invaluable, our two 'buddy' divers, Mosheko Bachar and Yair Bakal, and Naomi who worked with the dolphins and frequently came out with us to help attract them.

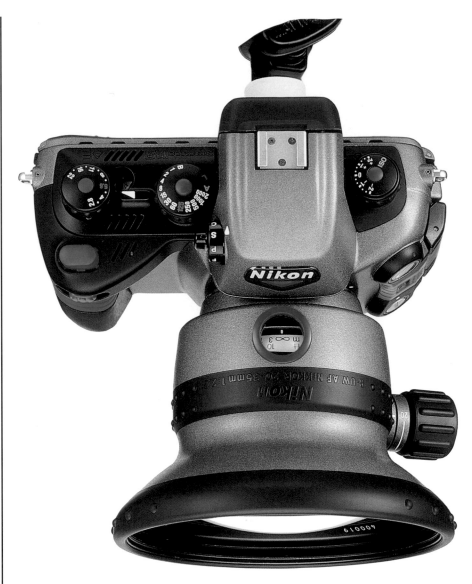

Top view of the Nikonos RSAF with 20mm-35mm zoom lens attached. This lens was used for nearly all the photographs in this book.

Having photographed water babies in the relative comfort of swimming pools, where I could sit easily on the bottom and generally have good visibility, I had to adjust my thinking when confronted with conditions under the sea. Visibility was not good when we arrived and shooting distances were initially hard to judge: what seems to be very close in the sea can actually be quite distant. As a result, my first shots were useless — I was too far away from my subject and it was underexposed. I had to get closer, so I swapped the 28mm lens — previously so good for the water babies — and switched to the zoom 20/35mm. I kept it on 20mm, which allowed me to get in closer — 1m (3ft) — and shot at TTL 1/125 at F11.

Having overcome these first few hurdles, I then had to surmount the enormous change and size in subject matter. The babies I had photographed previously had been quick and nimble in the water and confined to a relatively small space, but the bottlenosed dolphins who presented themselves to me were more like giant zeppelins torpedoing in and out of frame at a speed that I couldn't put a figure on. Unless they slowed down to be caressed, focusing was

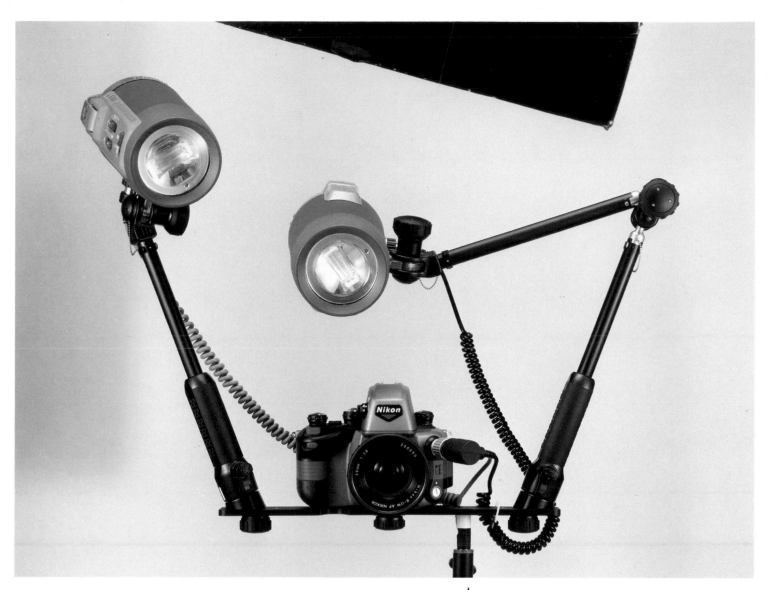

The Nikonos RSAF with SB104 flash unit attached.

problematic. The single auto focus on the camera had difficulty finding an area to focus on, probably because of the enormous shape in front of the screen, so I switched to the power focus mode with my finger pressed lightly on the shutter release. This allowed me to pan my shots with a little more control. The 20mm lens gave me a good depth of field, so I could be sure, more often than not, that when I was ready to trip the shutter, the image would be sharp.

Looking back on the project, I can truly claim that the RSAF camera was a joy to use and I became very attached to it. However, it must be said that it is very expensive, which puts it beyond the average consumer. But for those who, like me, love the idea of combining their diving skills with photography, the Nikonos V is an excellent substitute. It is cheaper, much lighter to carry and its optics, being Nikon, are second to none.

The other cameras used in the production of this book were my old but trusty Nikon FE and the Nikon HP F3, which I used with two lenses – the Nikonos 20/32 and the 28-85mm. Last but not least, I used the Hasselblad 500c with a 92mm portrait lens.

The black and white images seen in this book were taken on AgfaPan APX100. Most of the underwater and landscape sequences were taken on Agfa 100 Plus colour reversal film. Other photographs where light conditions were low, or where I wanted to achieve a particular effect, were taken with Agfachrome 1000 RS colour reversal.

Useful Addresses

AMERICAN COLLEGE OF NURSE MIDWIVES
818 Connecticut Ave. N.W.
Suite 900
Washington, DC 20006
Gives referrals to midwives throughout the U.S.

AUSTRALIAN SWIM SCHOOL
1202 Banbury Cross
Santa Ana, CA 92705
Infant swim programs for moms and babies as well as certification for instructors.

GLOBAL MATERNAL/CHILD HEALTH ASSOCIATION
P. O. Box 1400
Wilsonville, OR 97070
Provides water birth information, referrals, consultations, portable birthing pool rentals and sales, onsite workshops, and a waterbirth certificate course. The aquatic development program provides prenatal workouts and infant swim classes.

MATERNAL HEALTH SOCIETY
2045 Fraserview Drive
Vancouver, BC V5P 2N2
Canada
Sponsors water birth information and film showings, and rents portable birthing pools. MHS midwives have attended over 200 water births.

NATIONAL SWIM SCHOOL ASSOCIATION
1158 35th Avenue North
St. Petersburg, FL 33704
Holds conferences, publishes a newletter, and gives referrals to infant swim instructors across the United States.

Bibliography

CHAPTER 1: WHAT NEWBORN BABIES CAN DO
McGraw, M. B., 'Swimming Behavior of the Human Infant', *Journal of Pediatrics*, 15: 485-90, 1939.

CHAPTER 2: BABIES AND SWIMMING INSTRUCTORS
Kochen, C. L. & McCabe, J., *The Baby Swim Book*, Leisure Press, Illinois, 1986.

CHAPTER 3: BABIES AND PARENTS
Diem, L. *et al*, 'Langsschnittuntersuchung uber die Wirkung fruhzeitiger motorischer stimulation auf die Gesamtentwicklung des Kindes im 4-6', *Schriftenreihe des Bundesinstituts fur Sportwissenschaft*, Schorndorf, Hofman, 1980.
Pirkko, N., 'The Primary Steps in Learning', World Aquatic Baby Conference, UCLA, 1993.

CHAPTER 4: BABIES AND DOCTORS
Autti-Rämö, I., 'Handicapped Babies', World Aquatic Baby Conference, UCLA, 1993.
Goldberg, G. N. *et al*, 'Infantile Water Intoxication After a Swimming Lesson', *Pediatrics*, 70: 599, 1982.
Harter, L. *et al*, 'Giardiasis in an Infant and Toddler Swim Class', *American Journal of Public Health*, 74: 155, 1984.
Kropp, R. M. *et al*, 'Water Intoxication from Swimming', *Journal of Pediatrics*, 101: 947, 1984.
Pringle, M. B., 'Swimming and Grommets', *British Medical Journal*, 304: 198, 1992.

CHAPTER 5: PREGNANCY
Barker, D. J. P. *et al*, 'The Relation of Small Head Circumference and Thinness at Birth to Death from Cardiovascular Disease in Adult Life', *British Medical Journal*, 306: 422-6, 1993.
Barker, D. J. P. *et al*, 'Growth in Utero and Serum Cholesterol Concentration in Adult Life', *British Medical Journal*, 307: 1523-7, 1993.
Christiansen, O. B. *et al*, 'Study of the Birthweight of Parents Experiencing Unexplained Recurrent Miscarriages', *British Journal of Obstetrical Gynaecology*, 99: 408-11, 1992.
Koletzko, B., 'Transfatty Acids May Impair Biosynthesis of Long-chain Polyunsaturates and Growth in Man', *Acta Paediatrica*, 81: 302-6, 1992.
Law, C. M. *et al*, 'Initiation of Hypertension in Utero and Its Amplification Throughout Life', *British Medical Journal*, 306: 24-7, 1993.
Newnham, J. P. *et al*, 'Effects of Frequent Ultrasound During Pregnancy: A Randomized Controlled Trial', *Lancet*, 342: 887-91, 1993.
Tarantal, A. F. & Hendrickx, A. G., 'Evaluation of the Bioeffects of Prenatal Ultrasound Exposure', *Cynomolgus Macaque Teratology*, 39: 137-47, 1989.

CHAPTER 6: BIRTH IN A FEMALE ENVIRONMENT
Balaskas, J. & Gordon, Y., *Water Birth*, Unwin Hyman, 1990.
Huttunen, M. & Niskanen, P., 'Prenatal Loss of Father and Psychiatric Disorders', *Archives of General Psychiatry*, 35: 423-31, 1978.
Odent, M., *The Nature of Birth and Breastfeeding*, Praeger, New York, 1992.
Odent, M., 'Birth Under Water', *Lancet*, 2: 1476-7, 1983.
Odent, M., 'The Fetus Ejection Reflex', *Birth*, 14: 104-5, 1987.
Odent, M., 'Position in Delivery', *Lancet*, p.1166, 1990.
Simpson, E., 'Natural Pools of Clach Bhan on Ben Avon in the Cairngorms, *The Scots* magazine, April 1990.

CHAPTER 7: PLACEBO, HALO AND NOCEBO
Jarrett, R. J., 'Gestational Diabetes: A Non-entity?', *British Medical Journal*, 305: 37-8, 1993.
MacArthur, C. *et al*, 'Investigation of Long-term Problems After Obstetric Epidural Anaesthesia', *British Medical Journal*, 304: 1279-82, 1992.
Macaulay, J. H. *et al*, 'Epidural Analgesia in Labor and Fetal Hyperthermia', *Obstetrics and Gynecology*, 80: 665-9, 1992.
McCandish, R. & Renfrew, M., 'Immersion in Water During Labour and/or Birth: The Need for Evaluation', *Birth*, 20, 2: 79-85, 1993.
Odent, M., 'Birth Under Water', *Lancet*, 2: 1476-7, 1983.
Phillips, D. P. *et al*, 'Psychology and Survival', *Lancet*, 342: 1142-5, 1993.
Rosenthal, M. J., 'Warm-water Immersion in Labor and Birth', *The Female Patient*, 16: 35-47, 1991.
Rosevear, S. K., Fox, R. *et al*, 'Birthing Pools and the Fetus', *Lancet*, 342: 1048-9, 1993.
Viktrup, L. *et al*, 'Epidural Anesthesia During Labor and Stress Incontinence After Delivery', *Obstetrics and Gynecology*, 82: 984-6, 1993.

CHAPTER 8: LOVE, BIRTH AND WATER
Carmichael, M. S. *et al*, 'Plasma Oxytocin Increases in the Human Sexual Response', *Journal of Clinical Endocrinology and Metabolism*, 64: 27-31, 1987.
Odent, M., 'The Early Expression of the Rooting Reflex', *Proceedings of the 5th International Congress of Psychosomatic Obstetrics and Gynaecology, Rome*, Academic Press, London, 1977.
Odent, M., *Birth Reborn*, 2nd edition, Souvenir Press, London, 1994.
Odent, M., *Water and Sexuality*, Penguin, London, 1990.
Odent, M., 'Colostrum and Civilization', *The Nature of Birth and Breastfeeding*, Praeger, New York, 1992.

Pedersen, C. A. & Prange, A. J., 'Induction of Maternal Behaviour in Virgin Rats After Intracerebroventricular Administration of Oxytocin', *Proceedings of the National Academy of Sciences, USA*, 76: 661-5, 1979.

CHAPTER 9: WATER FROM BIRTH TO DEATH

Kujala, U. M. *et al*, 'Osteoarthritis of Weight-bearing Joints of Lower Limbs in Former Elite Male Athletes', *British Medical Journal*, 308: 231-4, 1994.
Panush, R. S. *et al*, 'Is Running Associated with Degenerative Joint Disease?', *Journal of the Americal Medical Association*, 225: 11-14, 1986.

CHAPTER 10: THE HEALING POWER OF WATER

Kitzinger, S., *Women's Experience of Sex*, Dorling Kindersley, London, 1983.
New York Academy of Medicine and New York City Public Health Committee, 'Maternal Mortality in New York City, 1930, 1931, 1932', The Commonwealth Fund, 1993.
Odent, M., 'Man, the Womb and the Sea: The Roots of the Symbolism of Water', *Pre- and Peri-natal Psychology Journal*, 3: 187-93, 1993.
O'Hare, J. *et al*, 'Observations on the Effects of Immersion in Bath Spa Water', *British Medical Journal*, 291: 1747-51, 1985.

CHAPTER 11: THE DOLPHIN CONNECTION

Balaskas, J. & Gordon, Y., *Water Birth*, Unwin Hyman, London, 1990.
Cochrane, A. & Allen, K., *Dolphins and Their Power to Heal*, Bloomsbury, London, 1992.
Dobbs, H., *The Magic of Dolphins*, Lutterworth Press, Guildford, 1984.
Dobbs, H., *Journey into Dolphin Dreamtime*, Jonathan Cape, London, 1992.
'Les Dauphins sauvent trois personnes', Reseau Cetaces No. 12, Paris, 1994.
Lilly, J., *Communication Between Man and Dolphin*, Julian Press, New York, 1978.
Smith, B., Using Dolphins to Elicit Communication from an Autistic Child', *The Pet Connection*, Minneapolis Center for the Study of Human-Animal Relationships and Environments, 1984.

CHAPTER 12: ARE WE MARINE CHIMPS?

Darwin, C., *The Descent of Man and Selection in Relation to Sex*, 2nd edition, John Murray, London, 1874.
Crawford, M. & Marsh, D., *The Driving Force*, Heinemann, London, 1989.
Morris, D., *The Naked Ape*, Jonathan Cape, London, 1967.
Nie, C. J. van, 'The Bulbous Aortae (*Aorta ascendens*) in the Growing Common Seal (*Rhoea vitulina vitulina*), *Aquatic Mammals*, 11, 3: 71-4, 1985.
Sibley, C. G. & Ahlquist, J. E., 'DNA Hybridization Evidence of Hominoid Phylogeny: Results from an Expanded Data Set', *Journal of Molecular Evolution*, 26: 99-121, 1987.

CHAPTER 13: WHEN HOMO BECOMES SAPIENS

Hardy, A., 'Was Man More Aquatic in the Past?', *New Scientist*, 7: 642-5, 1960.
Morgan, E., *The Descent of Woman*, Souvenir Press, London, 1972.
Morgan, E., *The Aquatic Ape*, Souvenir Press, London, 1982.
Morgan, E., *The Scars of Evolution*, Souvenir Press, London, 1990.

The World is too much with us, late and
   soon.
Getting and spending, we lay waste our
   powers:
Little we see in Nature that is ours;
We have given our hearts away, a sordid
   boon!
This Sea that bares her bosom to the
   Moon;
The winds that will be howling at all hours
And are up-gathered now like sleeping
   flowers;
For this, for everything, we are out of tune;
It moves us not — Great God! I'd rather be
A Pagan suckled in a creed outworn;
So might I, standing on this pleasant lea,
Have glimpses that would make me less
   forlorn;
Have sight of Proteus rising from the sea;
Or hear old Triton blow his wreathèd horn.

William Wordsworth, *Sonnet XVIII*,
September 1803

Acknowledgements

A project such as this cannot be achieved without the good-natured support of a large number of people. I am truly grateful to all the following:

The staff at Dragon's World, especially PIPPA RUBINSTEIN and HUBERT SCHAAFSMA who believed in the idea, and thus made this book possible, JOHN STRANGE who worked closely alongside me in the visual content and make-up of the book, MEL RAYMOND, LESLEY GILBERT, CAROLE KING and JULIE DAVIS, and TRISH BURGESS who edited the text.

ELAINE SWIFT and JOHN CLEMENTS of Nikon UK, who supplied the Nikonos RSAF and other Nikon lenses, and who gave me invaluable help and advice; MELVIN CAMBETTIE DAVIS, dear friend and excellent printer, and MAX FERGUSON at Master Mono, creative black and white printers; PAUL, PHIL and JOHN CASS of Cascolour Laboratories, who supplied quality prints and transparencies at a constantly fast turnaround; JOHN SABISTON, black and white retoucher; ED'S PHOTOSHOP at the Red Sea Sports Club Hotel, Eilat, Israel, for advice, help and processing; JOSEPH of Marina Photo, Eilat, Israel, for help, advice and processing; GUY VANBELLEGHAM of Professional Photographic Lab, Ostend, Belgium; WESTSIDE PROCESSORS, London; BRIAN GREEVES, ANNE BURGESS and MARIANNE GILBERT of Agfa-Gevaert Ltd, for supplying large quantities of film at short notice; and JONATHAN TOPPS at Fuji UK.

All the staff at Dolphin Reef, Eilat, Israel, especially NIR AVNI, General Manager, MOSHEKO BACHAL, Diving Manager and Lauren's buddy diver, YAIR BAKAL (Savvy), my buddy diver, NAOMI, MAYA, SHMULCK MASHRACH for help and advice, and his wife GAIL and her five lovely boys.

YVES DE SMEDT and ISABELLE GABRIELS, founders of Aquarius, for being the most generous of hosts; all the staff in the maternity unit of H. Serruys Hospital, Ostend, especially DR HERMAN PONETTE and DR JOHAN DESCHACHT, obstetricians, who allowed me to take photographs of several births, and DORINE, head midwife. Thanks also to DR JOHN MARIE for helping when my car broke down!

PETER BRICE and other helpful staff at Collins and Chambers who loaned me diving equipment; DR JOAN MARTIN and ERIC DILLEY of Kensington Emperors, plus all the parents, helpers and swimmers who allowed me to photograph the session; KATY and WILLIAM of Clarges in Brighton; JULIE and MICHAEL JOSEPH for use of the pool; and the curators at Bath.

Many people gave me help and advice. They include: MIKE PORTELLEY, who also introduced me to Lauren, PETER SCOONES, MARK SILK, DAVID SAUNDERS, JOHN TARRANT, who helped me start my waterbabies mission, BARRY LATEGAN, MICHAEL STEPHENSON and KITTY LAMBERS.

Special thanks to my family, FALCON, HUGO and DASHIELL, who have been so behind me during the course of this book and put up with long absences and a tired, work-obsessed mother. Thanks also to my dear mother, father and sisters CHARLOTTE and ROSALYNN.

Special thanks go also to DITTE DALKUIST OLSEN, who looked after my children during the four months spent working on this book. She was 'absolutely fabulous'. To ALICE BURTON, who also regularly helped and gave the boys fun days out – thank you. BETTY JACKSON, for allowing me to be present at the birth of JOSHUA and to photograph the happy event. Thanks also to all the maternity staff at King's College Hospital; REBECCA MEATON, true friend and regular helper with the boys and on numerous photographic shoots; LORRAINE DUNNE and her three beautiful water babies, SARAH, CLAIRE and RACHEL; BERNADETTE PIGGOT, for endless typing at short notice. To *all* my friends who have offered so much support and encouragement, I give warm and appreciative thanks in the knowledge that I couldn't have done this book without that back-up.

Finally, extra special thanks to LAUREN HESTON, who has constantly stood with me on all these projects and who has always put love and attention into every detail; to MICHEL ODENT for being a wonderful co-author and giving me much insight into the world of 'water babies'; and last but not least, all the men, women, babies and children who attended the shoots and who ultimately made this book possible.